Dare To Believe

Dan Baumann

G/L REGAL BOOKS

A Division of G/L Publications
Glendale, California, U.S.A.

The Scripture quotations in this publication, unless
otherwise noted, are from the *New American Standard Bible.*
© The Lockman Foundation, 1960, 1962, 1963, 1968, 1971. Used by permission.

The other version quoted is *TLB, The Living Bible,*
Copyright, © 1971 by Tyndale House Publishers, Wheaton, Illinois.
Used by permission.

Published by
Regal Books Division, G/L Publications
Glendale, California 91209,
Printed in U.S.A.

Library of Congress Catalog Card No. 74-53380
ISBN 0-8307-0516-3

Contents

Other Good Regal Reading

Cracking the God Code, by Michael Saward
Now that I'm a Christian, by Chuck Miller
The Christian Life: Issues and Answers, by Gary Maeder
 with Don Williams

To Steve and Lynette
Young in faith but,
along with friend-wife, Nancy,
"joint heirs with Christ."

Preface

This outline of Christian doctrine is sent forth with the hope that it may inform your mind, quicken your will and enrich your life. Doctrine, at its best, is to be lived, not simply defined. We need more of "theology in its work clothes" and "doctrine in its dungarees."

Let me hasten to express appreciation to Margaret Norrbom, who in the midst of her bout with cancer provided illustrations, texts to consider and suggestions regarding format.

Thanks also to Greg Vaughan who took my writings, sometimes "without form and void" and breathed clarity into the body of my book.

And, of course, as always my bride of 18 years took my dictation, worked with the rough drafts, and finally prepared a copy that we submitted to our friends at Regal.

These, and undoubtedly others, deserve much of the credit for any merit this work contains.

If God is pleased to use it in your life, it was worth all the effort, loss of sleep and pressure to meet deadlines.

Apostles' Creed

I believe in God the Father Almighty,
   Maker of heaven and earth.
And in Jesus Christ, His only Son, our Lord,
   who was conceived by the Holy Ghost,
   born of the Virgin Mary,
   suffered under Pontius Pilate,
   was crucified, dead and buried;
   He descended into hell;
   the third day He rose again from the dead;
   He ascended into heaven, and sitteth on the right
     hand of God the Father Almighty;
   from thence He shall come to judge
     the quick and the dead.
I believe in the Holy Ghost,
   the holy catholic church,
   the communion of saints,
   the forgiveness of sins,
   the resurrection of the body,
   and the life everlasting.

Amen.

Introduction

A number of years ago a best-selling book attempted to answer the question, "What can a man believe?" It was a good question then; it is a good question now.

It is my conviction that a book on basic Christian truths is sorely needed in our day. The reasons are readily apparent.

To begin with, there is widespread biblical illiteracy among Christians. Entrance exams in Bible at Christian colleges produce such incredible answers as: "The epistles were the wives of the apostles"; "Sodom and Gomorrah were husband and wife"; "We believe in three gods—Father, Son and Holy Spirit"; and "The Holy Spirit is an influence, not a person." Sunday School teachers, pastors and parents frequently feel like hanging their heads in shame at the lack of knowledge they discover in "their people."

Secondly, there is a tendency on the part of many enthusiasts to over-emphasize the experience of faith to the neglect of its content. As a result, the gospel is all but lost in impressionism. A "feeling theology." It *does* matter *what* a person believes. To be valid, theology must pass the truth test. Only then does it merit our allegiance.

Thirdly, it is our Christian responsibility to know what we believe. Paul's admonition is fitting for every Christian—"Be diligent to present yourself approved to God as a workman who does not need to be ashamed, handling accurately the word of truth" (2 Tim. 2:15).

Dr. Harry Ironside tells of a brilliant liberal preacher who pleased his audience with flowery oratory. At length he was called to another church. In his farewell discourse he stressed the importance of being broad in view and avoiding bigoted opinions. After the sermon, one of his young men approached him and said, "Pastor, I am so sorry we are losing you. Before you came I was one who did not care for God, man or the devil; but through your delightful sermons, I have learned to love them all!"

Fourthly, Christians need to know what they believe in order to share it with others. Peter said, "Sanctify Christ as Lord in your hearts, always being ready to make a defense to every one who asks you to give an account for the hope that is in you" (1 Pet. 3:15). Cult members know what they believe. Christians should settle for nothing less than the cultists do!

The Apostles' Creed

For the sake of this study, I shall use the Apostles' Creed as an outline. I do so because of its *universality.* You undoubtedly have some knowledge of the Apostles' Creed— even if you cannot recite it from memory. It is the best known of the available creeds or doctrinal outlines.

The Apostles' Creed is also marked by *simplicity*. It deals with a cluster of major truths in an understandable fashion. This is not always true of the options. All too often theological outlines are heavy, dull, and obscure. This, thankfully, is not the case with this statement of faith.

Furthermore, the Apostles' Creed is a truly *biblical* expression of Christian faith. Its adherence to the Scriptures is noteworthy. We would do well to follow its example in all of our statements.

The Apostles' Creed, according to historians, does not date back to the apostles but was composed in the first few centuries after Christ. It reached its present form about A.D. 650. Although it does not stem directly from the apostles, it is safe to say that it reflects the teaching of the apostles, as recorded in the Bible.

The Doctrine of the Scriptures

The Apostles' Creed is very basic, but we err if we think it is complete. The most glaring weakness is its failure to mention anything about the nature and purpose of the Bible. We need, therefore, to address that deficiency.

Every theology is built upon certain presuppositions. This work is no exception. A belief in the total infallibility of the Scriptures is foundational to the teaching in these chapters. By this I mean that no passage of Scripture will lead one astray in matters of faith, practice, history, geography or kindred sciences. Although the Bible is not intended as a science textbook, it is nonetheless scientifically trustworthy. The Bible, in its original manuscripts, was without error and, in its present form, is entirely trustworthy.

Scripture is inspired. In his last epistle, Paul told Timothy that "all Scripture is inspired by God" (2 Tim. 3:16). Scholars have generally maintained that "all Scripture" is a

13

reference limited in application to the Old Testament. I concur with John R. W. Stott who argues convincingly that it encompasses at least part of the New Testament as well. The context of 2 Timothy 3:16 gives direction to what is included in Paul's phrase, "all Scripture."

In 3:14, Timothy is encouraged to "continue in the things you have learned," namely the gospel taught by Paul. This word was given with apostolic authority. Reference is also made to "the sacred writings" which Timothy had known "from childhood" (3:15), namely the Old Testament Scriptures. Both sources of Timothy's knowledge are likely included in the statement of inspiration in 3:16.

To be sure, Paul does not call the Epistles "Scripture," but he comes close: (1) he professes to speak with authority from Christ, in His Name (2 Cor. 2:17; 13:3; Gal. 4:14); (2) he calls his message "the word of God" (1 Thess. 2:13); (3) he claims to be taught by the Holy Spirit (1 Cor. 2:13). These statements are tantamount to a claim of verbal inspiration. In addition, the apostle Peter regarded Paul's letters as Scripture when he called the Old Testament "the rest of the Scriptures" (2 Pet. 3:15,16).

The word "inspired" (2 Tim. 3:16) is a conjunction of two Greek words "God" and "breathed." The Scriptures were "breathed out" by God. These were not existing documents upon which God "breathed"; they were brought into existence by the Spirit of God. This truth is stated succinctly by Peter, "Men moved by the Holy Spirit spoke from God" (2 Pet. 1:21). In this process of inspiration human individuality was not destroyed, it was maintained. The writers of Scripture spelled out the truth of God, consistent with the expressions of their own personality, with the superintendence of the Holy Spirit guaranteeing their utter reliability.

Scripture is profitable for salvation. "All Scripture is . . .

profitable" (2 Tim. 3:16). The Bible is a book of divine origin for human profit—it is *from God* and *for man!*

The Bible is primarily a book of redemption. In this "handbook for salvation" we discover the heavenly Father's program for our initiation into the family of God. The Scriptures "are able to give you the wisdom that leads to salvation through faith which is in Christ Jesus" (2 Tim. 3:15). The Old Testament with its sacrificial system is preparatory for the New Testament message of Christ, His death and resurrection.

Jesus Christ is the source of salvation and faith is the instrumentality chosen by God to make it a personal experience (see John 3:16, Acts 4:12, and Eph. 2:8,9). Inasmuch as all are sinners (Rom. 3:10,23), it is imperative that this message be shared with the entire world (Acts 1:8). The purpose of Scripture is obvious in this regard. Unless we had had this revelation of divine purpose, we never would have known how to be right with God.

Scripture is profitable for creed. The problem of spiritual dropouts is often related to a lack of understanding regarding the content of Christian theology. We have all known of so-called Christians who have gone back into the world "Demas fashion" (see 2 Tim. 4:10). Over and over again the pattern is predictable. A person professes faith in Christ and is immediately ushered onto the platform for a testimony. One thing follows another and before long the person is in the limelight—receiving recognition, given a position of responsibility and inevitably a prime target for Satanic attack. The downfall is tragic. The person starts well but is soon spiritually profligate.

Two decades ago, a Canadian evangelist followed this pattern. He was a gifted pulpit man with obvious gifts of persuasion. He did not, however, have much theological

15

foundation for his ministry. When he recognized the deficiency, he began reading different theologians. Some of the writers were liberals, others were neoorthodox. His own faith began to falter. At length he realized that his personal statement of faith was inadequate. When he recognized his theological uncertainty, he left Christian work and entered the entertainment field in Canada.

A mature Christian faith must be built upon a solid theological foundation. Before anyone is qualified for leadership, he needs to learn the grace of worship and be disciplined in the verities of biblical truth.

The Bible is "profitable for teaching, for reproof" (2 Tim. 3:16). The first is positive (i.e. doctrine), the latter is negative (i.e. the refuting of error or the exposing of heresy). Foundational to all mature Christianity is the bedrock of a theology that is both thorough and comprehensible—a system of truth that discerns what is and what is not the teaching of the Scriptures. When this does not happen people are prey for the cults and spiritual disaster. All too frequently, religious people, with only a smattering of biblical understanding, are swept into Mormonism or Jehovah's Witnesses. For the first time in their life they do some studying. Unfortunately, it is the "false words" (2 Pet. 2:3) of a destructive heresy.

We may well conclude that the reason the "hallelujah crowd" on that first Palm Sunday had dissipated in five days (Good Friday) was that they had built their experience on a foundation of sand. Enthusiasm is no substitute for a thoughtful theology. They, and we, stand in need of a faith with definition. The Bible exists for this purpose.

Scripture is profitable for conduct. Paul instructed his son in the faith, Timothy, that "all Scripture is . . . profitable . . . for correction, for training in righteousness" (2 Tim. 3:16). Not only is the Bible a source book for doctrine, but it is equally profitable for an informed life of godliness. Its message is intended to transform a man's thoughts, motives and actions. This has been called "doctrine in its dungarees."

"Correction" means to "set right." The Bible, when applied to the individual, will issue in the reformation of life. How often Christians testify to the power of God's Word to define a problem and then illumine the way in which it can be overcome. This applies to such areas as acts of purity and morality, as well as to attitudes of envy, covetousness and pride.

"Training in righteousness" is the positive instruction contained in Scripture which defines the nature of a life of active obedience. Right living is a natural consequence of living in the Word. There are no shortcuts to holiness. If you desire to live a life that pleases God, you must regularly search the Scriptures for truths that beg for implementation.

Every autobiography of notable Christians documents this truth. The godliness of a George Muller, Hudson Taylor or David Livingstone is no accident of history. It is the result of disciplined study of the Bible, God's Word. As one person commented, "The best binding for a Bible is not morocco, it is human flesh."

In order to maximize your experience with the doctrines in this volume, you should keep your Bible open before you. Read the passages and ask the Spirit of God who inspired the truth to illumine it to your understanding. In the final analysis our desire should be the sentiment expressed in a simple chorus learned in childhood, "The B-I-B-L-E, yes that's the book for me. I stand alone on the Word of God, the B-I-B-L-E."

1. Faith Needs to Be More than Fashionable

"I believe..."

It is fashionable for people to talk about faith these days. Talk shows on radio and TV feature this form of discussion and magazines frequently publish stories about the philosophy of life espoused by well-known actors, athletes and politicians. Although this pattern is commendable, much of this discussion ought to make us apprehensive. You should note some of the weaknesses found in contemporary faith.

Faith Needs a Definite Object

It is not unusual to hear such statements as: "I believe in the potential of man"; or, "I believe in the ultimate victory of good." While these are not necessarily wrong, they err in the direction of sweeping generalities. They say very little.

The most deficient statements I have ever heard were expressed in a midwestern newspaper interview with a well-known public figure who said, "I believe in faith" and then added, "It doesn't make any difference what a man believes so long as he is sincere." Tell that to a man who has gotten on a plane piloted by a chimpanzee! Faith is meaningless unless it is placed in a worthy concept or person. Faith must have a definite object or it becomes an airy figment of the imagination.

Faith Does Not Equal "Success"

There is a strange teaching abroad in America these days. Its most perverse form is expressed by Reverend Ike. He chants with the enthusiasm of a used car salesman that we should "seek first the Kingdom of God and His righteousness and ALL THESE THINGS WILL BE ADDED UNTO YOU." He then proceeds to enumerate "these things"—a trip to Paris, a fur coat, a Cadillac, a new home, etc. Most apostles of the "Gold in God" cult are not quite so crass. You will discover, however, after you strip away their clever rhetoric that Christian faith and success *are* equated. Pressed to its logical conclusion this means that the wealthy are giants of faith whereas the poor are agnostics, atheists and unbelievers. Such a conclusion is, of course, ridiculous.

The Bible never suggests that the man of faith will automatically prosper in material things. Faith and financial success are not synonymous. In fact, there is much to document the opposite truth.

Faith Is More than a "Feeling"

When faith is dependent upon the mood of the individual, one is committed to a roller coaster experience.

When things go well, faith is strong. When adversity comes, faith bottoms out.

A young lady from a midwestern city had built her salvation on her moods. One day when she felt depressed she ran away from home feeling that all was lost. She simply felt empty about God, the Bible and Christianity. And, because she felt empty, she concluded her salvation had vanished. A few days later, however, she returned when her mood changed and she felt better. This "roller coaster" of faith is an experience familiar to many.

Faith will vacillate when it is built upon something as unreliable as our feelings. From the biblical vantage point, faith is rooted in the character of God and His truth. We have a know-so salvation not a feel-so salvation. John wrote, "He who has the Son has the life; he who does not have the Son of God does not have the life. These things I have written to you who believe in the name of the Son of God, in order that you may *know* that you have eternal life" (1 John 5:12,13 italics added).

Before we go further it is well to define our terms. Faith, writes the author of Hebrews, is "the assurance of things hoped for, the conviction of things not seen" (Heb. 11:1). Edward John Carnell, the former president of Fuller Theological Seminary (Pasadena, California), in his lectures to students frequently stated that faith is "a resting of the mind in the sufficiency of the evidence." He meant by this that the heart should only believe what the head approves. The point is that faith is reasonable—it is not contrary to reason. For a working definition of faith call it "confidence or trust in a person or thing."

What Does the Bible Say About Faith?
Faith is important, but it is not the greatest Christian grace.

The position of "greatest" is reserved for love. "But now abide faith, hope, love, these three; but the greatest of these is love" (1 Cor. 13:13).

Faith may exist in larger or smaller measure. You can see this truth in the life of Abraham. As the patriarch grew older it seemed, humanly speaking, that he would never see the promise of an heir fulfilled. And yet, even though he was a hundred years old and his wife Sarah's womb was considered "dead," it is recorded that Abraham "did not waver in unbelief, but grew strong in faith, giving glory to God" (Rom. 4:20).

Robert Schuller, Pastor of the Garden Grove Community Church (California), is a modern-day example of an individual living by faith. Through his unswerving confidence in God, he has been enabled to challenge individuals to donate huge sums of money to the ministry of his church! In less than a period of six months, he saw four individuals promise to give one million dollars each to God's work in Garden Grove.

A dynamic grace which may exist in small measure, faith has the potential for growth and expansion. Take a typical evangelical congregation as a case in point. The membership is made up of people who believe in Jesus Christ. As such, they are the people of faith. But, and this takes no stretch of the imagination, it is clear that some members have great faith, some have moderate faith and a relatively large number could be included in the "O ye of little faith" group. Faith, we would insist, exists in all of them; equal amounts of faith do not.

With an understanding of this reality comes the incentive for increasing our faith. No one is locked into a certain level of faith. Abraham's faith continued to grow, and so can ours.

Weak faith can be strengthened by the Lord. At the outset

of His public ministry Jesus selected a group of 12 men to accompany Him. They appeared to be a group with little potential—unlearned, sometimes impetuous, and frequently deficient in understanding.

After Jesus expounded to the multitudes He sometimes found it necessary to have tutorial sessions with the Twelve; they simply did not comprehend His methods or His message. One would think that Jesus should have despaired with that motley crew, but the patience of the Master is a wonder to behold. He continued to model the truth, to teach the truth and occasionally to have "bonehead review" with the dull apostles.

The Saviour's confidence in them proved, after a time to be well deserved. How else can you explain the name of "Rock" given to Peter who still resembled Jello? It must have encouraged Jesus when the apostles, who acknowledged the weakness of their faith, said to the Lord, "Increase our faith!" (Luke 17:5). The full answer to that request came almost like a time bomb to 11 of the apostles at the time of Pentecost. Small faith became large faith—a gift from their Lord.

Anything, in the will of God, that will bless and strengthen the Christian is potentially available to the believer. As a youth I was scared stiff to speak in front of people. Through the encouragement and prayerful support of my parents, I was enabled to see that my gift—though undeveloped—was preaching. Today, I delight in the privilege God has given me to preach His Word every single Sunday. God is good. He can take the tender tissue of fear and turn it into the strong muscle of faith. The prerequisites are two in number—a recognition of need and a confidence in the ability of the Lord to do what He promises (see Heb. 11:6).

The opposite of faith is worry. In Luke 12:22-32, "men of little faith" are those who are anxious about their life, what they shall eat and what they shall wear. After all, says the Lord, "life is more than food, and the body than clothing" (v. 23). He continues, "If God so arrays the grass in the field, which is alive today and tomorrow is thrown into the furnace, how much more will He clothe you, O men of little faith! And do not seek what you shall eat, and what you shall drink, and do not keep worrying" (vv. 28,29).

To worry is an evidence of small faith. An evidence of large faith is a stance of rest on the part of the Christian. There is a clergyman of my acquaintance who was a veritable beehive of activity—always busy, sometimes fretful, frequently tired and generally anxious. He was encouraged by a friend to take a good look at himself, and today he is a different man. His ministry is healthy and his own personal life is marked by more faith than ever before. He is a man who has learned to relax (not a synonym of laziness) in the Lord realizing that his frantic activity added nothing tangible to God's work. He discovered in practice what Luke 12 is all about: If we "seek for His kingdom . . . these things shall be added to you" (v. 31). Concern about the future is legitimate, anxiety is a lack of trust.

Real faith affects behavior. Martin Luther in his enthusiasm for the truth of "the just shall live by faith alone" denied the canonicity of the book of James. He called it "a right strawy epistle" because it seemed to be at odds with the theology of a works-less salvation.

We can understand Luther's dilemma. He had such emotional ties to the doctrine of justification by faith alone that he could not sit back objectively and see that the message of Romans and Ephesians is really quite compatible with that of James. For example, a careful reading of

James 2:14-22 teaches that real faith makes a difference in the life of the believer. To put it another way, if I told you that I loved my wife but never showed her any kindness, affection or attention, you would be justified in calling me a liar. True faith expresses itself in works. Jesus said that a man's commitment is expressed in the quality of his life. (See Matt. 7:16.)

One thing which separates Christians from demons is their style of life. Mark it well—"the demons also believe" (Jas. 2:19). Christians should live a life which is qualitatively different because real faith affects behavior. Words and creeds do not prove faith but a changed life does.

Faith found a new focus after the resurrection of Christ. Prior to the redemptive events of Calvary and the empty tomb, faith was essentially trust in God the Father. As you read through the Old Testament and the pre-Calvary narratives you discover that faith is trust in God and the reliable character of what He promised. The shift takes place with the discovery of the vacated tomb. From that point forward faith was placed in Jesus Christ. (See Acts 2:32,33; Rom. 4:24,25; 1 Pet. 1:20,21.)

Faith today is placed in Jesus Christ. To trust solely in God the Father is to be in the position of the Old Testament saints who did not have the benefit of God's final revelation in the person of His Son, Jesus Christ.

Faith for salvation is a gift of God. Not only is salvation a gift of God, but the very faith which makes it possible is also a gift. Ephesians 2:8 teaches that "you have been saved through faith; and that not of yourselves, it [faith] is the gift of God."

God's movement towards man is always primary. He provides the faith as a gift of His grace. E.C. Blackman summarizes: Faith "is man's initial awareness of God and also a continuing attitude of personal trust in God. God's movement toward man is primary; the initiative is with God. But there must be the corresponding movement on the human side and this is basically what is meant by faith. For this reason, the importance of faith cannot be over-emphasized."[1]

Why Is Faith Necessary for Everyone?

There is no alternative. No one can honestly call himself an unbeliever. Every man chooses a philosophy around which he organizes his life. Even materialists, the humanists, agnostics and atheists are believers. They have chosen something that governs their lives. Faith, even though it is placed in untruth, is nonetheless faith. The typical atheist vigorously believes that love of humanity is a higher love than a love of God. He will say in effect, "Praying to God is humiliating; worshiping God is degrading." Yet, atheists and numerous other forms of non-Christians are "believers."

The question at stake is not "Are you going to believe?" It is, rather, *"What* are you going to believe?" or, *"In whom* will you place your trust?"

No man has ever lived who was not a believer of some sort. Unfortunately, millions have not chosen to place faith in the proper object. Faith, only when placed in Jesus Christ as object is truly Christian faith.

Belief determines destiny. One day Joshua gathered the rebellious people of Israel together and asked them to choose whom they would serve (see Josh. 24:15). It was either the gods of this world or the Lord God. Joshua and his family chose the Lord. Each person's decision determined the destiny of his eternal soul.

Sometime later Elijah gathered the chosen people together on Mount Carmel for a showdown of faith (see 1 Kings 18). The awesome sight included thousands of Israelites and 450 prophets of Baal. It was a long day for the pagan leaders as they begged their gods to send fire to the erected altar. The accompanying mockery of a confident Elijah was no help, in fact it must have angered them to the boiling point. At length Elijah had his turn. He rebuilt the altar, thoroughly drenched the sacrifice with water and called down fire in a colorful demonstration of faith. Prior to these dramatics Elijah (to quote Peter Marshall's sermon "Trial by Fire") said, "If the Lord is God, follow Him; but if Baal is God, follow him . . . and go to Hell!"[2]

One midnight in a cold, damp Philippian prison two men, Paul and Silas, were singing. This is incredible when you realize that they had recently been beaten with rods and then placed in stocks. Only a man's reliance upon God can lift him above such circumstances. In the midst of this God sent an earthquake that rocked the prison and severed the chains binding the prisoners.

The jailer, assuming everyone had fled and his own life was at stake, prepared to commit suicide. He was halted by the strong, authoritative voice of the apostle Paul which rang through the fractured walls of the prison, "Do yourself no harm, for we are all here!" (Acts 16:28). Trembling with fear, the jailer fell at the feet of God's servants and asked the question of ultimate significance, "What must I do to be saved?" (v. 30). Paul's reply revealed the secret of eternity, "Believe in the Lord Jesus, and you shall be saved" (v. 31). It is still the same today. By faith in Jesus Christ a man can establish beyond doubt the eternal destiny of his soul.

The familiar passage from John's Gospel says that "whoever believes in Him should not perish, but have eternal life" (John 3:16). An act of faith determines whether a man will spend eternity with God or an eternity separated from God. Viewed in these ultimate terms, faith becomes more than a luxury. Our eternal destiny hangs in the balance.

Blaise Pascal's famous "wager" puts it something like this.

If I bet there isn't a God,
And there isn't—nothing gained, nothing lost.
And there is—eternal loss.
If I bet there is a God,
And there isn't—nothing gained, nothing lost.
And there is—eternal gain.[3]

Even to those unenlightened by the authority of God's Word, this makes logical sense. How much more it means to those of us who accept the authority of Scripture. As Jesus said to Martha, "I am the resurrection, and the life; he who believes in Me shall live even if he dies" (John 11:25).

Faith is an anchor for here and now. In a world continually beset by uncertainty in government, in economics and in resources; in a world that heaves with unrest; in a day when heartache is a universal phenomenon—you need some stability. Faith in Jesus Christ is God's plan for such a time. Rather than "whistling in the dark," you can find a certain anchor for your life in one who is the "same yesterday and today, yes and forever" (Heb. 13:8).

Faith for the Christian takes two distinct forms—"saving faith" and "serving faith." Saving faith is that act of resting in Jesus Christ for salvation. This can generally be pinpointed in time. It represents a time when the individual, sensing his need of salvation and his separation from God, turns over his life in a personal commitment to the Saviour. God the Father honors that faith in His Son and through the Holy Spirit works the miracle of new life. Then the words of 2 Corinthians 5:17 make sense, "If any man is in Christ, he is a

28

new creature; the old things passed away; behold, new things have come."

Recently I conducted a funeral for Doyle, a 58-year-old man who had given his life to Christ about a year ago. Prior to his conversion, his two daughters and wife had been born again. Only two members of his immediate family, his son and daughter-in-law were without salvation.

On Monday, two days before Doyle died, the son asked to see me. We sat in a vacant waiting room of the hospital and talked.

He began by saying, "My dad wanted me to be born again before he died, could we do something about that?"

What a privilege it was to rehearse the plan of salvation and then listen as Wayne prayed to ask Christ into his life. I walked with him into the intensive care unit to see his dying father.

Wayne stroked his father's fevered forehead, bowed close to Doyle and said, "I love you, dad, and I want you to know I just gave my life to Jesus."

His father could not speak, but he gave a knowing squeeze of the hand and breathed a sigh of relief. It was a moment I will never forget.

At about midnight on the same day I had the privilege of seeing Kathy, Doyle's daughter-in-law, put her faith in Christ. When the funeral service came it was a time of coronation—all the family knew Christ and dad was in the presence of the Lord. That is what *saving faith* is all about!

Serving faith is that growing reliance on the Lord which enables an individual to meet the demands and pressures of daily living. This differs from saving faith in that it is a dynamic experience which finds expression in a variety of ways. It cannot be easily pinpointed in time. It is not so much an event or moment in time as it is a life-style.

29

When Jesus was preparing to return to the Father, it created a great deal of unrest in the hearts of the 12 men who left everything to follow Him. It was necessary for Jesus to comfort them, "Let not your heart be troubled; believe in God, believe also in Me" (John 14:1). Faith in Jesus was a promised source of support and comfort.

A friend of mine watched his wife go through a mental breakdown. It was obvious that he felt very deeply the pain of her suffering. His concern never slackened. Yet, in the midst of it, his spirit was one of victorious reliance. He knew the Lord and could rest in the truth that "My grace is sufficient for you, for power is perfected in weakness" (2 Cor. 12:9). God proved Himself faithful—He always does!

The testimony of Christians for 1900 years is that God can be trusted—whether for salvation or for daily needs. Take Him at His word—He is trustworthy!

Additional Scriptures
for Study About Faith and Believing
Mark 9:17-24
John 3:1-18,36; 5:19-24; 6:31-40; 12:44-46; 20:26-31
Acts 10:38-43; 13:38,39
Romans 9:30-33; 10:5-17
2 Timothy 3:14-17
1 John 5:1-13

Footnotes

1. George A. Buttrick, ed., *The Interpreter's Dictionary of the Bible*, vol. 2 (New York: Abingdon Press, 1962), p. 222.
2. Peter Marshall, "Trial by Fire."
3. Blaise Pascal, *Pensees* (New York: E.P. Dutton & Co. Inc., 1954), pp. 65-70.

2. God Is for Real

"I believe in God the Father Almighly, maker of heaven and earth."

"God is dead!" That's what a group of theologians told us just a few years back. Predictably that so-called "theology" died, but God Himself lives on. The God of the Bible, the God of the Christian Church, the God of the believing heart, is alive and well!

I am sure you have been struck with the profound simplicity of the opening words of the Bible, "In the beginning God . . ." (Gen. 1:1). The Bible's magnificent first words speak volumes. There is no attempt to prove God. The Scriptures, from Genesis through Revelation, assume His existence. There is no attempt to defend faith in God. The evidences appear too clear to the biblical writers. There is no attempt to persuade people to believe in God. The Scriptures assume that persuasion is quite unnecessary;

not to believe in God is sheer foolishness (Ps. 14:1).

Unfortunately, millions have not allowed the Bible to be their teacher. As a result, there are a number of options—all inadequate—for the true God.

Atheism—God Does Not Exist

Madelyn Murray O'Hair is a present-day atheist. You perhaps know her through her opposition to Christian broadcasting, or her campaigns against prayer in public schools. She frequently gets involved in radio and TV debates. She has debated with folks like youth evangelist Jack Wyrtzen and theologian John Warwick Montgomery. Her position is clear—there is no God.

Some people are atheists because of the moral argument. These atheists cannot accept the fact of God in the light of troubling evidences around them. They argue, How can you believe in God when there are wars which kill thousands and maim thousands more? What about Vietnam, Korea, World War II, World War I, etc.? How can you believe in God when there are famines in Bangladesh? How can you believe in God when a tornado dips its ominous power to earth and destroys life? How can you believe in God when 21,000 are killed in an earthquake that rocked Guatemala? How can you believe in God when a sweet, beautiful 18-year-old girl dies from the dreaded enemy, cancer?

These are tough questions, and there are no easy answers. All the tragedies in our world point to the plague of sin.[1] Nothing has escaped the ravages of sin. No one has eluded the impact of sin. It is in this kind of a world that we need God.

Some people are atheists because of the psychological argument. These atheists argue that God is a creation of man. Because individuals needed something to depend on they concocted a God. Man's crutch is called "God." He is a necessary prop.

The Bible declares that "the fool has said in his heart, 'There is no God' " (Ps. 14:1). Atheism is not only foolish, it is imposing. The atheist assumes for himself what he denies for God. For you see, an unbelief in God's existence demands omniscience (all knowing), omnipresence (everywhere present at once) and eternity as a bare minimum. The atheist, to be *certain* of his position, must have roamed all nature and found no divine footstep anywhere. He must have investigated into the knowledge of all existing spirits in the universe and found no God. The atheist must also have gone back into time to check out all previous evidences.

It seems, then, that the atheist's position can be rather precarious, but some of those who deny God's existence do live noble lives. "Why is it," a friend once asked Phillips Brooks, the learned Boston preacher of the nineteenth century, "that some of these men who call themselves atheists seem to lead such moral lives?"

"They have to," was the reply. "They have no God to forgive them if they don't!"

Only a small minority of people in the Western hemisphere are theoretical atheists. Very few would *say* that they do not believe in the existence of God. Many, however, including Christians, live as if God did not exist. Their attitudes, behavior, and thought life give no evidence that God is part of their conscious experience. While theoretical atheism affects a few, practical atheism affects a majority of the population.

Agnosticism—I Do Not Know if God Exists
The agnostic says he does not know if there is a God. In a sense, this is more intellectually respectable than the position

33

of the atheist. The agnostic, at least, has left the door ajar.

When we ask questions like: Where did life begin? Who or what is the author of the first one-celled animal? How do you account for the regularity in nature? Or, what happens after death? The agnostic must respond with a shrug of the shoulders.

The evidences all around us—Bible, nature, philosophy, personal experience—deem agnosticism unnecessary. A decision can be made. "The evidences demand a verdict."

Theism—GOD Is

As I said earlier, the Bible nowhere attempts to prove God. The Bible *assumes* God. It does not argue for His existence. There are, however, some suggestions, though not final proofs that we can consider.

Our intricately planned world could not have come into being by chance alone. It takes more faith to believe that our world came into being by accident than it takes to believe that it was created by God! This belief is the *cosmological argument.*

Years ago I read of a man who said that there were 19 parts to a meat chopper. He mentioned that you could put those 19 items in a wash tub and shake them around for millions of years—they would never reassemble themselves and make a meat chopper. How much more incredible to believe that this world assembled itself without a guiding hand! Even Voltaire, the sceptic, confessed, "If God did not exist, it would be necessary to invent Him."

There must be a God (i.e. a cause) *to account for the sense of right and wrong within every man.* No anthropologist has ever discovered a culture anywhere in our world that did not have an awareness of good and/or duty. Sometimes, to be sure, that awareness has expressed itself in some strange ways, but the awareness is universal. This argument for the existence of God is the *moral argument*.

Kant, the philosopher, said that there were two things that never ceased to amaze him: the starry heavens above and the moral law within.

In the final analysis, the most convincing argument for the reality of God is the testimony of those who know God, the argument from *experience.* You can argue with philosophical reasoning, but it is much more difficult to refute a life that is changed through an experience of God.

The songwriter says, "You ask me how I know He lives, He lives within my heart." Or, as a bumper sticker expressed it, "God is not dead. I talked to Him this morning." I believe in God for many reasons—it makes the most sense, it is taught by Scripture, and I know Him personally. God is—I have experienced Him!

In most of the opinion polls conducted in America, 90-95 percent of the population claims to believe in God. It is obvious, however, that not all theists have a true, biblical understanding of God.

You, no doubt, have met some of the contemporary caricatures that attempt to pass for God:

1. *The Resident Policeman.* God is a nagging inner voice. Just about the time you want to enjoy yourself, He blows the whistle. At worst He "spoils our pleasure and at best keeps us rather negatively on the path of virtue."[2]

2. *Parental Hangover.* If your parents are kind, so is your God. If, however, your parents are severe and fearful, so is your God. God becomes a whip-carrying disciplinarian who can't wait for us to miss devotions so that He can punish us.[3]

3. *Grand Old Man.* God is pictured as a gray-haired, smiling old gent in a rocking chair. He is a nice old fellow, but He is not "with it." He is kind of an archaic remnant of

the past, who talks in King James English. He does not understand a nuclear age.[4]

4. *God-in-a-Box*. God must be a member of my denomination. If I am a Baptist, so is God. If I am a Presbyterian, Methodist, or you name it, so is God. If God were to visit our town He would, of course, attend our church and no other. God-in-a-Box is a provincial deity who is bound by my limited perspective.[5]

5. *Santa Claus*. God is an eternal disperser of gifts. His function is to satisfy the selfish requests of earthlings who are perpetually asking. God is viewed primarily as a giver.

6. *Great Computer*. God is a heavenly machine, about as personal as an IBM computer. He is mechanical, cold, and impersonal. He neither knows me nor loves me.

The God of the Bible Is Different

If we want to really know who God is, we must discover where that truth has been revealed. Assuming that God has chosen the Scriptures as the primary means of revelation, then the Bible becomes our primary source of information. What does the Bible say about God?

God is a personal Spirit. God is not what someone has called an "oblong blur." He is alive, personal and involved with His creation. Genesis 1:26,27 teaches that we were made in "the image of God"; in other words, there are parallels between His personhood and ours. Not the least of these parallels is His ability to relate meaningfully to us and we to Him. Contrary to the teaching of some cults, God the Father is spirit (John 4:24). He does not possess a body. Only Jesus, the Son of God, chose to express Himself in bodily form (Col. 2:9). God the Father is a spirit who can and wants to be involved with us.

God is eternal. Time is a category that has particular

36

meaning to human beings. We might ask each other, "How old are you?" The question implies a beginning. If you were to ask me I would reply, "I was born November 5, 1933 in the Ravenswood Hospital, Chicago, Illinois." I did not exist until 1933. My life began in 1933.

God is different. The Bible says, "In the beginning God . . ." (Gen. 1:1) and, "In the beginning was the Word and the Word was with God, and the Word was God" (John 1:1). This means, of course, that both God the Father and God the Son are without beginning. They were in "the unbegun beginning."

We are so accustomed to thinking of persons and things that have a cause, a beginning. God had none. He was. He was not caused. Past, present, and future are terms that apply to us, not to God.

If you were to board a small plane and fly above the highway on a holiday, you would see the highways choked with traffic. Such a view would allow you to take in the whole situation. But suppose you were transferred to one of the cars. Immediately time and space would take on a decidedly different meaning. You would be part of the stop-and-go parade that seldom moves faster than 10 miles an hour. You would have no understanding of the total traffic situation.

God is "in the plane" all the time—always has been and always will be. He sees the whole scope of time in a single glance. Time is a limitation of man. God is not limited—He is eternal.

God is the Creator. The world we live in is the creation of God. To be sure, we have polluted and destroyed much of earth's beauty, but the original version was God's masterpiece.

We do not know with any degree of certainty when the

world was created. That is a subject for the geologists to ponder. Their educated guesses are instructive and helpful. The purpose of Scripture is not to pinpoint the time of creation nor even the process. Far more important is the question of *who*, not how or when. The Bible majestically states, "In the beginning God created the heaven and the earth" (Gen. 1:1). God has revealed Himself in the Bible and in creation. "The heavens are telling of the glory of God; and their expanse is declaring the work of His hands" (see Ps. 19:1).

God's revelations are not contradictory, and we can be free to allow the scientists to help us understand the world. True science should also help us interpret the Scripture teaching on creation. Each should help us interpret the other.

As I write this section I am enjoying a visit with my parents in beautiful Door County, Wisconsin. It is apparent to me that only God could create such magnificence! The blue water of Green Bay, the straight, clean lines of the white birch trees, the smell of evergreen, the rock formations assembled into lofty bluffs and the star-spangled sky at night—who else but God!

This universe is an eloquent expression of God's craftsmanship. I don't know who said it but the truth remains— "God doesn't have to put His signature on the sunset, for no one else could paint it!" Our universe with all its order, magnitude and intricacies is inexplicable without God. We worship a God who made it all!

God is everywhere. Theologians use the term "omnipresent" to express the fact that God is everywhere present at once. Read Psalm 139 and allow the psalmist to stretch your understanding. There is no place where God is not present!

The God of the Bible can at the same moment in time be

with the worship service of hundreds packed into a Baptist Church in Moscow, with three Chinese meeting in a secret Bible study, with a humble Ethiopian dresser assisting an American doctor in Addis Ababa, with a blind elderly widow in Seattle reading Psalm 91 in braille, and right there with you wherever you are.

How foolish is the story of Jonah. As you probably know, Jonah was a prophet of God. It was his calling to know God and to declare His truth. One day God commissioned him to go to Nineveh and preach a message of repentance. If they failed to respond, their city would be destroyed. Jonah was not happy with the prospect of Assyrians receiving God's grace; as a matter of fact, he was downright rebellious! So, he went to Joppa to board a ship that would carry him across the Mediterranean Sea to Tarshish.

And, you recall, God sent one whopper of a storm after this rebellious, pouting prophet. Jonah should have known better. He feebly attempted to flee "from the presence of the Lord" (Jon. 1:3), which is impossible. No runaway teen, military man, unfaithful wife or bitter senior citizen has ever been able to find a place where God was not. This truth is both a challenge (to be what God wants me to be) and a comfort (He is with me regardless of my location).

God is holy. The word "holy" found in Isaiah 6:3 comes from a Hebrew word which means "to separate." God is separate from sin; He is without defilement; He is absolutely pure. Little wonder then that Isaiah responded in awe when he met God, "Woe is me, for I am ruined! Because I am a man of unclean lips" (Isa. 6:5).

We forget this truth in some of our folksy type of Christianity. A number of years ago *Time* magazine carried an article about a trio of Hollywood starlets who had gotten "religion." Each in turn told of her faith. Jane Russell, one of

39

the three, said that God was such a close friend that she called him "Daddy." I was troubled when I read that. Perhaps you feel the same way. God is loving and personal, but we err when we drag Him down and make Him "the man upstairs" or "Daddy." We need the corrective of Isaiah who saw the Lord for Who He is—a holy God who deserves our worship.

A flippant relationship to God is irreverent. It also encourages a life that does not take sin seriously. The more we know about God's holiness, the less we will allow sin to go unchallenged and unforgiven in our life.

God is love. Shout it from the housetops, "God will never love me more than He loves me right now." For, you see, God's love is total and unconditional. I can never earn more of His love. He is showering total love upon each of us right now.

If you are ever tempted to question God's love, let your imagination take you back to the Garden of Gethsemane where Jesus wrestled with the problem of bearing our sins, follow Him to that rugged hill, watch the soldiers as they drive wooden spikes into His hands, hear the tearing of flesh as they jar the cross into the ground, listen to the insults thrown at the Galilean, watch the spittle drip from His face as the mockers pay their unholy disrespect. Calvary says it like nothing else could—God loves me (John 3:16). We read simple but profound words in 1 John 4:8, "God is love."

God's love is not selfish (*eros*), nor simply brotherly (*filial*), but freely and abundantly given to undeserving people like ourselves (*agape*).

In a recent World Series, Charles Finley, the impetuous owner of the Oakland Athletics, became enraged when Mike Andrews, his second baseman, made two errors in one game. According to reporters he secured a physician's report on

40

some so-called problem which he used to keep Andrews on the bench.

When the series moved to New York, Felix Millan, the second baseman of the Mets made an error. Immediately after the game the reporters crowded around the Mets' manager, Yogi Berra, to see how he would handle that situation.

Reporters said, "Finley benched Andrews, what are you going to do to Millan?"

Without a moment's hesitation, Berra replied, "I wish every ball were hit to Felix Millan."

I am grateful that God is more like Berra than Finley; He loves me and that gives me confidence to live a life that is more pleasing to Him. God's love is constant, unconditional and enabling.

To sum it up, what kind of a God have you been honoring? Have you created a god in your own image? A god who does not demand much, a god who is an unworthy object of your worship? Or, have you been smitten by the reality of God's Word and yielded to the biblical God? Here indeed is a God worthy of our utmost praise and devotion. "God the Father Almighty, maker of heaven and earth" is a God in whom we can trust!

**Additional Scriptures
for Study About God the Father**
Genesis 1
Deuteronomy 32:6
Nehemiah 9:5,6
Job 12:7-12; 26:7-13
Psalms 24; 65; 95; 104
Isaiah 45:11,12; 64:8
Malachi 2:10

Matthew 7:11; 23:9
Romans 3:29; 8:14-17
1 Corinthians 8:5,6
Ephesians 4:4-6
1 Peter 1:13-17

Footnotes

1. The reader is encouraged to read C.S. Lewis, *The Problem of Pain* (New York: Macmillan Company, 1955) for a helpful discussion of this knotty issue.
2. J.B. Phillips, *Your God Is Too Small* (New York: Macmillan Company, 1955), pp. 9-23.
3. Phillips, pp. 14-19.
4. Phillips, pp. 19-23.
5. Phillips, pp. 37-41.

3. What Difference Does It Make Anyhow?

"I believe in ...Jesus Christ His only Son, our Lord; who was conceived by the Holy Ghost, born of the Virgin Mary."

During a lecture at an East Coast graduate school of theology, I heard the nationally-known pastor of a large downtown church make an unusual confession. He said that he could no longer recite the Apostles' Creed at his own church services when a particular assistant was worship leader. The problem, he noted, was that the assistant pastor "believed the Apostles' Creed was *literally* true." The gray-haired clergyman went on to suggest that the doctrines of the virgin birth and resurrection of Jesus were particular problems for him. The Apostles' Creed, according to this self-professed "liberal," was a poetic expression; certainly not a statement full of literal, historic events.

43

It should be at once obvious to you that I feel differently. The Apostles' Creed was originally intended to be a statement of faith. Each phrase is to be taken as historically true. This certainly applies to the section which affirms the virgin birth of Christ. Christians have always believed that Matthew 1:18-25 and Luke 1:26-38 describe an essential element in the "invasion" of planet earth by our God. God became man—through the miracle of virgin birth. This doctrine, explicitly taught by the Scriptures, has been opposed by some, but it is an essential dimension of historic Christianity.

The Virgin Birth Is Taught in the Scriptures

Biblically-based doctrine on the virgin birth of Christ is not a recent invention of theologians. It did not arise out of man's creativity nor is it a post-biblical tradition. It is part of biblical revelation, a clear-cut teaching of the Scriptures.

Isaiah 7:14 is the classic Old Testament prophecy of the virgin birth: "Therefore the Lord Himself will give you a sign: Behold a virgin will be with child and bear a son, and she will call His name Immanuel." The word translated "virgin" is the Hebrew word *almah*. This Hebrew word can be translated "young woman," "maiden" or "virgin." Because Matthew 1:23 quotes Isaiah 7:14, and used the Greek word for "virgin" (which allows for no other meaning), it is clear that the proper way to translate *almah* is "virgin." The best commentary on Scripture is Scripture. The clue to understanding Isaiah 7:14 is given to us by Matthew 1:23.

Two New Testament passages teach the doctrine of the virgin birth. Matthew 1:18-25 views the story from Joseph's perspective. Joseph, who was betrothed to Mary, discovered that his bride-to-be was pregnant. Being a righteous man, he felt some action was necessary immediately. He had an obvious moral problem on his hands. One can well imagine that Joseph tossed and turned in his bed at night thinking of a proper way to save Mary from disgrace and also to protect his own reputation.

Before proceeding further in the story, we would do well to recall that there were three steps to a Jewish marriage. Step one was the engagement in which a committal similar to twentieth-century engagement was made between a man and a woman. Step two was betrothal. Americans have no parallel to this in their marriage ritual. It was a time in which a man and the woman were expected to avoid sexual relations with each other and yet in order to break betrothal it was necessary to secure a form of divorce.

Step three was the marriage ceremony itself. Joseph and Mary had reached the second stage but were not yet united as husband and wife. Her pregnancy, therefore, suggested that there had been an impure sexual relationship between Mary and Joseph or Mary and some other man.

One night while Joseph was seeking a solution to Mary's moral problem, an angel of the Lord appeared to him, "Joseph, son of David, do not be afraid to take Mary as your wife; for that which has been conceived in her is of the Holy Spirit." The angel went on to say of the coming child, "You shall call His name Jesus, for it is He who will save His people from their sins" (Matt. 1:20,21). With this clear assurance from the Lord Himself, Joseph arose from his bed and did as the angel of the Lord had instructed him and married the woman to whom he was betrothed.

The second New Testament narrative, Luke 1:26-38, teaches the doctrine of the virgin birth from Mary's perspective. It is recorded that the angel, Gabriel, came to Nazareth, a small city in Galilee, and appeared to Mary. He said, "Hail, favored one! The Lord is with you" (v. 28). Understandably, Mary was startled at such a statement; she could not figure out what it was the angel was trying to tell her. Noting her consternation, the angel comforted her, "Do not be afraid, Mary; for you have found favor with God. And behold, you will conceive in your womb, and bear a son, and you shall name Him Jesus" (vv. 30,31).

If the virgin birth was a moral problem for Joseph, it was even a greater problem for Mary. As a pure young Jewish maiden, a virgin by conviction and practice, conception was a biological impossibility. The angel clarified the purpose of God by saying, "The Holy Spirit will come upon you, and the power of the Most High will overshadow you; and for that reason the holy offspring shall be called the Son of God" (v. 35).

These two passages, Matthew 1:18-25 and Luke 1:26-38, constitute the only clear teaching in the New Testament of the virgin birth doctrine. The two narratives, one from Joseph's perspective, and the other from Mary's perspective, are clear and not difficult to understand.

In the history of mankind God has only had four ways in which He has made human bodies, three of which are miraculous.

Adam's body was made without the agency of man or woman. Genesis 2:7 says, "The Lord God formed man of dust from the ground, and breathed into his nostrils the breath of life; and man became a living being." We know nothing more than what the text reveals. God created man out of something that was lifeless and breathed into it life. The well-known poet, James Weldon Johnson, describes the event very graphically when he tells of God going down to the river bed, taking mud, forming it into a man and then breathing into it His own life. The poet describes God as simply saying, "I am lonely. I'll make me a man."

In actuality, we can only guess what the Bible leaves unsaid.

Eve's body was made with the agency of just a man. Genesis 2:18 the Lord God said, "It is not good for the man to be alone; I will make him a helper suitable for him." And so God the Father made the beasts of the field, the birds of the sky. They were brought to Adam and he gave them names. But among them God did not find a suitable helper. God the creator then caused "a deep sleep to fall upon the man, and he slept; then He took one of his ribs, and closed up the flesh at that place. And the Lord God fashioned into a woman the rib which He had taken from the man, and brought her to the man" (Gen. 2:21,22).

Many writers have enjoyed playing with this narrative. With a twinkle in his eye one author says that "God took the rib out of man to make woman; however, it seems more likely that he took his backbone." Another author, perhaps more seriously but with the same poetic license, remarks that God did not take a bone from the head of Adam so that woman would be above him; nor a bone from Adam's foot so that she would be below him—but a rib so that woman would stand by his side. Whether there is any validity to that interpretation or not, it remains true that man and woman stand side by side as equals because of God's creation.

*Every person born into our world has come into being through the agency of both man and woman—*WITH ONE EXCEPTION. This natural, God-ordained way is the way you and I received our bodies.

Jesus was conceived and born through the agency of just a woman. The Holy Spirit fertilized the egg in the miraculous conception of Jesus Christ.

When Mary conceived, she was pure and unmarried (Matt. 1:18). The *fertilization* was a supernatural act. The

47

birth itself was natural. There is no indication in the Scriptures that Mary gave birth to Jesus any other way than through natural procedure. Later on she had other children such as James. There is no biblical reason to believe in her "perpetual virginity."

The Virgin Birth Is Denied by Modernists

Some choose to believe that the virgin birth teaching is unreasonable. Harry Emerson Fosdick, the well-known leader of modernism in the 1930's, said, "I am not deeply concerned whether you believe the virgin birth as an historical fact or not. Although, as you know, I cannot believe it."[1] It just seemed incredible to Fosdick.

H.G. Wells, the noted historian said, "We should strip the Gospels of the birth of Jesus, the star that led the wisemen, the massacre in Bethlehem and the flight into Egypt. They are evidently accretionary in nature. Such miraculous events are unreasonable and peculiar."[2]

Some believe that it is simply a biological impossibility; it just does not happen in the world of scientific reality. Some choose to believe that the Bible writers simply included an idea they received from ancient folk tales. While it is true that there are tales of supernatural births in ancient mythology, there is not a single instance in mythology of a son born to a virgin. In almost all of these myths the narrative is full of immoral and gross activity, and nothing at all like the reverent, moral and simple teaching of Matthew and Luke.

Some moderns refuse the doctrine of the virgin birth because they feel the biblical evidence is weak. Bruce Barton said that the virgin birth theme did not concern Jesus and because this creed had no authorization from Christ Himself it could not be a part of the teaching of the Christian church.[3]

It is true that the rest of the New Testament is silent on this doctrine of virgin birth. John, Peter and Paul say nothing about it. This prompted Charles Reynolds Brown, the former Dean of the Divinity School of Yale University, to comment, "When anyone asks me what do you say about the virgin birth, I usually reply, I say just what Paul said. He did not say anything. In all of his recorded letters and sermons not a syllable about the virgin birth . . . I am quite content to stand where Paul stood."[4]

Indeed, Paul does not mention the doctrine of the virgin birth. But then again, he does not make any parental reference at all. Matthew and Luke mention it. How many times must a doctrine be taught in order for it to be true? Paul never denied it; he had other purposes in his writing. We do well to remember that the Beatitudes are only mentioned in Matthew, yet Brown and others have no difficulty in accepting them. It seems that these men are guilty of taking what they want to believe and refusing what they choose not to believe. The very fact that the doctrine of the virgin birth is taught in only two New Testament books is insufficient evidence for Bible believers to reject it. On the contrary, it gives us two reasons to accept it.

If you choose to reject the virgin birth of Jesus Christ, what are the alternative theories?

1. Jesus was the legitimate child of Joseph and Mary (Ernest Renan, the French skeptic).[5]

2. Jesus was the child of a German soldier and Mary. Nels Ferré, the Harvard educated Swedish theologian wrote, "Nazareth was hard by a Roman garrison where the soldiers were German mercenaries. Jesus is also reported throughout a continuous part of the history of art to have been blond . . . hence Jesus must have been the child of a German soldier! . . . Such is the experience of many girls near military camps."[6] How is that for blasphemy?

49

3. The virgin birth story is of pagan derivation. Some have said that the disciples borrowed the virgin birth idea from well known Greek stories which gave the gods unusual births. In the believers' enthusiasm for their Master, they added a miraculous birth to the otherwise true statements regarding Jesus' life.[7]

The Virgin Birth Is Basic

Biblical authority accepts the virgin birth. Second Timothy 3:16 and 17 teaches that all Scripture is given by inspiration of God. If you deny the stories in Matthew and Luke, you play havoc with the infallible claims of Paul. All of the Scripture is authoritative and inspired. If a truth is taught only once, it is as true as if it were reiterated time and time again. It is not possible to believe in an infallible Bible and at the same time deny the virgin birth. Once you accept the Bible's statement about its own nature, you must of necessity accept its teaching on the miraculous birth of Jesus Christ.

The eternity of Christ demands it. John 1:1 says that "In the beginning was the Word, and the Word was with God, and the Word was God." No natural union of husband and wife could ever bring into the world an individual who had lived previously. Inasmuch as Christ was pre-existent, a unique birth was necessary.

The sinful nature of natural man requires it. Romans 5:12 teaches that sin entered into the world and spread to all men. If Christ was not virgin born, then He was born as other men, conceived in sin and He Himself needed a saviour. Jesus was the perfect Lamb of God who was born without original sin and lived without actual sin. Only a virgin birth, superintended by the Holy Spirit would sidestep the problem of the curse of sin that plagues men.

Redemption demands it. In order for Jesus to become the

50

redeemer, it was necessary that He take on human form. He could not die for other men unless He Himself was a man. In order to also be the Messiah, He had to be born through the line of the house of David. Through the supernatural means of the virgin birth, He was both man through Mary and God through the Holy Spirit. If He were a typical man, He would be a sinner and could only pay for Himself. But as the God-man, He could identify with both God and man and take the sins of the world on Himself. His death on Calvary and His resurrection from the Garden Tomb combine to provide the divine means whereby the virgin-born redeemer could pay the penalty for the sins of the world and provide redemption to all who believe.

In conclusion, Jesus was a living miracle. He was sinless, the provider of miracles. He conquered the grave through resurrection. He exited from the world by ascension and, according to God's own word, He entered the stream of our humanity by the miracle of the virgin birth. With millions of Christians for 20 centuries, I believe "in Jesus Christ His only Son, our Lord; who was conceived by the Holy Ghost, born of the Virgin Mary."

Additional Scriptures
for Study About Jesus the Son of God
Matthew 3:13-17; 8:28,29; 14:22-33; 16:16; 17:1-5
Mark 1:1
John 1:9-14, 29-34; 3:16-18; 10:33-38; 11:25-27
Acts 9:17-20
Hebrews 10:26-29
1 John 4:9-15

Footnotes

1. Harry Emerson Fosdick, *Riverside Sermons* (New York: Harper & Row Publishers, 1958), p. 271.
2. H.G. Wells, *The Outline of History* (New York: Macmillan Company, 1924), p. 498.
3. Bruce Barton, *What Can a Man Believe?* (Indianapolis: Bobbs-Merrill Co., 1927), p. 206.
4. Charles Reynolds Brown, *Where Do You Live?* (New Haven: Yale University Press, 1926), p. 111.
5. Ernest Renan, *The Life of Jesus* (New York: Carleton, 1864).
6. Nels Ferré, *The Christian Understanding of God* (New York: Harper & Row Publishers, 1951), p. 191.
7. See J. Gresham Machen, *The Virgin Birth of Christ* (New York: Harper & Brothers Publishers, 1930), pp. 317-379.

4. What Is So Good About Good Friday?

"I believe in …Jesus Christ…who suffered under Pontius Pilate, was crucified, dead and buried; He descended into Hell."

When my son, Steve, was in junior high he asked the question, "Why is it called Good Friday? Why not Bad Friday?" Good question. If it were not for the doctrine of redemption taught in the Bible and the fact of Easter morning, it would indeed be "Bad Friday."

The story in Scripture is one in which a seeming tragedy is a triumph and defeat is actually victory. God through Christ made a cruel event into one of the most exciting events in the history of mankind. Jesus did not die a martyr's death. He died for our sins, a fact which makes Good Friday really *good.*

The Preparation for Jesus' Death

The Old Testament foreshadows the work of Calvary. Genesis 3 tells why sin entered the arena of human history. Adam and Eve were placed in a garden. Only one restriction was placed upon the original pair—God told Adam and Eve that the fruit of the tree in the middle of the garden was to be left untouched. The penalty was simple enough: if they ate from the tree, they would die.

One day Satan used a serpent to tempt the garden dwellers. Not only did the serpent mock God's commandment regarding the tree, but he said dogmatically, "You surely shall not die! For God knows that in the day you eat from it your eyes will be opened, and you will be like God, knowing good and evil" (Gen. 3:4,5).

The woman who was alone when approached by the serpent thought to herself, "It really does look good to eat" and she took of it and ate.

We, of course, do not know what forbidden fruit it was, whether the traditional apple, or a pomegranate, or whatever. The point is that Eve disobeyed God. She gave also to Adam and he ate, and together the two plunged themselves into the heretofore unknown realm of sin. Ever since that day Satan has lured men to act selfishly in defiance of God's command.

In Genesis 3:15 we have the first biblical prophecy of an opponent for Satan: "And I will put enmity between you and the woman, And between your seed and her seed; He shall bruise you on the head, and you shall bruise him on the heel." Many Bible scholars believe that this verse teaches that the seed of woman, namely Jesus, shall bruise Satan.

Later in Genesis 4:1-5 we read the story of Cain and Abel, the children of Adam and Eve. These first children brought offerings to God; one was acceptable, the other was rejected.

Cain, the farmer, brought of the fruit of the ground. God refused to accept it. Abel, a keeper of flocks, brought a slaughtered animal. God accepted his offering. Here we see the beginning of a pattern that is to carry us straight to Calvary: without the shedding of blood there is no acceptable offering for sin. Cain and Abel must have been informed regarding this either by God directly, or indirectly through Adam and Eve.

Exodus 12:21-27 rehearses the establishment of Passover. Moses told the elders of Israel that they were to kill a passover lamb and that the blood from this lamb was to be applied on the doorposts and lintel of each house. That night the Lord passed over the land of Egypt and killed the first-born of every family. But in every home where there was blood on the lintel and doorposts, life was spared; that is, when blood was applied, God reacted mercifully.

When I was in seminary my wife, Nancy, made a wreath of greenery, red ribbon and two Styrofoam canes. It was placed on the front door of our apartment as part of the Christmas decorations. One of our neighbors, a little five year-old named David, was fascinated by the decoration, and without thinking he broke off both Styrofoam canes.

That night his mother gave him a bath. The symbolism of coming clean evidently got to his little heart and he confessed his "life of sin." The next day his mother came to our door dragging a somewhat reluctant five-year-old son. When Nancy answered the door, David's mother looked at her son and said, "What are you going to tell Mrs. Baumann?"

David barely looked up and mumbled, "I broke your canes and I am sorry."

David's mother was attempting a reconciliation of David, the sinner, and Nancy, the sinned-against one. Atonement,

55

which occurs when a sinner gets right with the sinned-against one, creates an "at-one-ment."

God, of course, is the One against whom we have sinned and atonement must take place if that sin which separates us from a holy God is to be disposed of. "For the life of the flesh is in the blood, and I have given it to you on the altar to make atonement for your souls; for it is the blood by reason of the life that makes atonement" (Lev. 17:11).

This particular verse, Leviticus 17:11, provides the principle of atonement and sacrifice. The Old Testament preparation for the death of Christ, which we have come to call the sacrificial system, was based upon four principles: (1) failure in man is recognized; (2) reconciliation of the guilty to the offended party is necessary; (3) demands of the offended party (namely God) have to be met; and (4) an innocent substitute for a guilty person must be provided.

Many lambs that lived in Old Testament times became the innocent victims of sacrifice slaughter because of human sin. Such lambs were to be spotless, a foreshadowing of Jesus Christ, the Lamb of God who took away the sin of the world.

The Proceedings Surrounding Jesus' Death

The four Gospels, Matthew, Mark, Luke and John, unfold the drama leading to Calvary. Jesus, according to historians, was born about 4 B.C.[1] His birth was humble, in a barn in Bethlehem. At the age of 12 His superior wisdom and interest in God's work were evident in His conversations with the rabbis in the temple. At age 30 Jesus left the carpenter's shop of His family to mingle with people, teaching as no one else had ever taught: preaching repentance and the Kingdom of God and healing the sick. The blind were made to see, the deaf could hear, the crippled

56

made to walk again. Even the dead were raised and given new life.

At the age of 33, Jesus, knowing what was ahead, made His way to Jerusalem for the final countdown to His death. He went to the garden of Gethsemane where, forsaken by His disciples, He fought all alone the last great battle before the cross. Ahead lay the cross and crucifixion.

Crucifixion, we should be reminded, was a form of punishment reserved by the Romans for slaves, foreigners and the vilest of criminals. It could not be inflicted on a Roman citizen. Not only that, but crucifixion was not a part of Jewish law. Deuteronomy 21:23 and Galatians 3:13 teach that "cursed is every one who hangs on a tree." It was the cruelest and most hideous form of punishment used in that time.

The trial of Jesus Christ was fixed; illegal in both time and process. Two nights of trial were required by law, but the opponents of Christ rushed it through in a single evening. Trumped-up charges were brought against Him. Pilate, the Roman official in charge of the proceedings, tried to appease Christ's accusers. He felt he could handle the problem by offering the swelling crowd a choice between freeing Jesus or the convicted robber, Barabbas. Pilate assumed that law-abiding people would want Jesus freed; and that the robber, Barabbas, would get what he had coming. But Pilate underestimated the mob-mentality of the crowd that night, and was forced to release the robber and to sentence Jesus to death.

Jesus, sentenced to die by crucifixion, next endured a bloody scourging by Roman soldiers, who raked His back with iron-tipped thongs. Others had died as a result of the scourging before they ever reached the cross. Jesus' back was undoubtedly shredded as He made His way to Calvary hill,

57

burdened with the weight of His instrument of death, the cross.

Crucifixion was the most painful method of public death in the first century. The victim was placed on a wooden cross. Nails, undoubtedly wooden, were driven into the hands and feet of the victim, and then the cross was lifted and jarred into the ground, tearing the flesh of the crucified and racking his body with excruciating pain. Historians remind us that even the soldiers could not get used to the horrible sight, and often took strong drink to numb their senses. There were six hours of anguish on the cross before Jesus died, at 3:00 P.M.

The twentieth century has forgotten how cruel and hideous crucifixion really was. We have perhaps unwisely and sometimes unconsciously glamorized the cross. Jewelry and steeples alike are often ornamental and attractive and carry nothing of the real story of crucifixion.

Why, we ask, did the Jews demand His death? The Jews with one accord looked forward to a Messiah, the anointed one. He would be like David their king (Hos. 3:5). He would rebuild as in the days of old (Amos 9:11) and He would come to subdue the powers of evil (Ezra). Jesus did not fulfill this picture (Mark 9:31,32) and many of the Jews left Him because of this. A suffering Messiah was unacceptable to the rabbis who had applied Isaiah 53 to the nation of Israel, "not to a *messianic* person." Jesus, therefore, was a blasphemer. He must die.

But unconsciously, they were doing the work of God. Jesus came into the world for that purpose—to die. They were playing "right into God's hands!"

The Purpose for Jesus' Death

The purpose of Christ's death was redemptive, a story of

salvation and atonement. Before I look at the basic doctrine of atonement, I invite you to consider two popular inadequate theories of atonement.[2]

One of these is the ransom theory. Origen and Augustine, among others, taught that a ransom was paid to Satan in order to deliver man from his grasp. The problem with that theory is that Satan doesn't own us. While it is true that some sell out to Satan, it is God who owns His creation. The ransom was paid to God who demanded that a sufficient price be paid. It doesn't make much sense to pay Satan if he didn't own us in the first place.

The second is the moral theory. Horace Bushnell, an influential nineteenth-century theologian, said that the cross has a moral effect on the hearts of men. When man views the cross, something good happens to him, his character changes. This theory fails to sufficiently recognize the holiness of God and the sinfulness of man. If God is holy, as the Scriptures tell us, He is something far more than just a moral movement that occurred at Calvary. The Word of God provides a more helpful clarification of the answers we seek.

The meaning of Christ's death unfolds in four steps.

The first step, Christ had to die because of the sin problem: Romans 3:23 says, "For all have sinned and fall short of the glory of God." This is bad news. If it had not been for the garden of Eden and the fall of man, Calvary would have been unnecessary. However, before we are tempted to blame Adam, we must recognize that we unquestionably would have done the same thing. Man is not only a sinner by character, but by personal choice. Adam messed it up at the start—we have been messing it up ever since. Sin has left its ugly smudge on all of us.

Some years ago I was driving down a freeway in Minneapolis. Two ladies were in distress. Their car was stalled and the hood was up. Panic was written on their faces. I stopped to play Good Samaritan. Fortunately, the problem was very elementary. The fan belt had become dislodged and I was able to put it back in place. I still recall my self-congratulations as I drove from that scene. "My, what a fine Christian I have just been." Obviously, pride had ruined the whole thing. Often, it seems, when we do the right act, we sin in attitude.

The second step, Christ had to die because of the sin penalty. Romans 6:23 says, "For the wages of sin is death," and this, too, is bad news. Not only am I a sinner, but eternal separation from God is what I deserve. God keeps the records. He knows that I have sinned, and because He is holy and just, I must be paid accordingly.

In 1952 I worked for my Uncle Gust as cherry orchard boss in Sister Bay, Wisconsin. The cherry pickers were paid 25¢ a pail. These folks knew all the tricks! They would kick in the bottom and cover it with cherries, mix small branches among the fruit, or leave stems among the cherries.

It was my responsibility to make sure that the cherry pickers were giving us 25¢ worth of cherries in every pail. Uncle Gust was not going to pay 25¢ for ¾ or ⅔ of a pail of cherries. They were to get what they earned—no more and no less.

The parallel is simple enough. Every one of us is a sinner. We know it and God knows it. The penalty for our sin is spiritual death; namely, eternal separation from God. And we deserve it.

The third step, Christ had to die to provide a solution for sin. Hebrews 9:22 says, "And according to the Law, one may almost say, all things are cleansed with blood, and without shedding of blood there is no forgiveness," and this is good news. Man cannot make atonement. Many have tried by being religious, going through all the forms of worship and sacraments, baptism, communion, giving the tithe, serving on committees, singing in the choir, teaching Sunday School classes and the like. All of the religious activity in the world will not bring God and man together.

Others have given to charity. They give large gifts to hospitals or needy organizations. It is a fine gesture to give money to the cancer fund, but it will not bring a person one inch closer to God, who has been alienated by our sin.

Others have tried kindness. Somehow they feel that if they are good enough and kind enough that God will be obligated to let them into His heaven. It is all inadequate, for only God Himself can atone for sin. The blood of an innocent man must be shed. Christ died to pay the debt of our sin.

The fourth step, Christ had to die as the sinner's substitute. Romans 5:8 says, "But God demonstrates His own love toward us, in that while we were yet sinners, Christ died for us." The very good news of the gospel is that Jesus took our place. He was my substitute. I am guilty but He took my place. Barabbas probably had the best idea of atonement of anyone on Good Friday. He knew he deserved crucifixion and that Christ should have been released. But instead the door of the prison swung open and Barabbas departed as a free man. I imagine that he went to Calvary to see the man who was dying. He probably worked his way through the crowd and looking up into the face of Jesus remarked, "I do not know who you are, but I know you are there in my place."

Each one of us like Barabbas could go to that place of the cross and say, "I know you are there in *my* place." Because Jesus died we may live. This is the gospel, the good news.

The Descent into Hell

The curious phrase "He descended into hell" that follows after Christ "was crucified, dead and buried," has given interpreters of the Apostles' Creed a field day. The classical two volume work by Alfred Edersheim, *The Life and Times of Jesus the Messiah,* denotes less than one paragraph out of some 1600 pages to this concept.[3] I am tempted to follow suit. But your curiosity, as well as mine, encourages me to say more.

Bible students have taken the phrase to mean a number of things. One interpretation is that this is another way whereby our Lord would provide a second chance for our salvation—even after death. He will go even to hell itself to offer His grace.

Another interpretation is that this is an image picturing Jesus Christ bursting into even the darkest regions as victor and conqueror. It portrays the completeness of the Saviour's victory. I cannot support either of these interpretations, particularly the first.

Without making it a test of orthodoxy, the interpretation that best appeals to me is one that views Christ's descent into hell as part of the price He paid to purchase salvation for those who believe. Not only, I propose, did Jesus become sin for us (see 2 Cor. 5:21 and 1 Pet. 2:24), but He tasted all the cursed consequences of sin in our place, even hell. No wonder Jesus cried, "Eloi, Eloi, lama sabachthani?" "My God, My God why hast Thou forsaken Me?" (Mark 15:34). The rightful end of man is hell, that is, a place of banishment from God. Jesus Christ, if this suggestion is valid, not only became sin for us, but He also tasted the consequences of sin. It was this act of love which provides the way for us to escape hell by faith in the One who has already been there. He experienced sin, death and hell in our place. He is thereby enabled to offer us victory over sin, the gift of eternal life and the promise of heaven.

So, why is Good Friday so good? Simply this: God took the worst event, the most hideous, cruelest of all punishments and made it into the most blessed event of mankind. Through an ugly cross and the crucified Saviour, God provided our great salvation.

That is what is so good about Good Friday.

Additional Scriptures
for Study About the Death of Christ
Isaiah 50:6; 53
John 10:11-18; 12:23-28
Romans 14:9
1 Corinthians 15:3,4
Revelation 5:9

Footnotes

1. See the historical discussion in John B. Davis *A Dictionary of the Bible*, 4th edition (Grand Rapids: Baker Book House, 1954), p. 380.
2. Augustus Hopkins Strong, *Systematic Theology* (Westwood, New Jersey: Fleming H. Revell Company, 1954).
3. Alfred Edersheim, *The Life and Times of Jesus the Messiah*, 2 vols. (Grand Rapids: Wm. B. Eerdmans Publishing Company, 1956), 2:612.

5. The Most Incredible Fact in History

"I believe...in Jesus Christ...the third day He rose again from the dead."

Author Josh McDowell says, "After more than 700 hours in studying this subject and thoroughly investigating its function, I have come to the conclusion that the resurrection of Jesus Christ is one of the most wicked, vicious, and heartless hoaxes ever foisted upon the minds of men, or it is the most fantastic fact of history."[1]

McDowell is right. The resurrection of Jesus Christ cannot be treated with neutrality. The claim of resurrection is so vast and far-reaching that either it is the greatest deception or the greatest single fact in history.

Think about it! Jesus lived. Of course He did. Jesus died. Of course, He would have to. Jesus rose from the dead. Wow! That is difficult for modern man to believe. It strays from rationality. A belief in the resurrection of Jesus Christ is a *faith* commitment. But this belief is based on significant evidences.

There are three reasons for believing in the resurrection: The tomb was empty; Jesus Christ appeared to His disciples; the lives of the disciples were transformed.

The Tomb Was Empty

Jesus was crucified on Friday and placed in the tomb of Joseph of Arimathea. On Saturday, the Jewish Sabbath, the women rested. On Sunday morning, as recorded in the narrative of Luke 24:1-12, the women went to the tomb. The air was brisk at that early hour and the ground was still wet with dew as they came to anoint the bandages and complete the work of embalming. When they arrived (v. 2) the stone covering the grave had been moved. No explanation, just the statement. So the women entered the tomb (v. 3). When they did this, they met angelic visitors who "stood near them in dazzling apparel" (v. 4). The angels announced, "He is not here, but He has risen. Remember how He spoke to you while He was still in Galilee, saying that the Son of Man must be delivered into the hands of sinful men, and be crucified, and the third day rise again" (vv. 6,7).

You may recall that when these words were spoken, Peter had commented, "God forbid it, Lord! This shall never happen to You" (Matt. 16:22). The message of Jesus had fallen on unbelieving ears. Either His words had not been taken seriously or else they were forgotten. How often we, too, hear biblical truth and it makes no impression or is quickly forgotten.

The Reverend Caleb Morris was a British preacher who retired due to ill health. He went, however, and conducted services in a convalescent home week after week. As he stood before his congregation of 20 to 30 elderly people he would ask about the previous week's message. If it had been forgotten, he would preach it over again!

Jesus had the same problem with His disciples. He kept instructing them regarding His death and His resurrection, and those closest to Him either misunderstood or they forgot it almost immediately. The ladies, with the assistance of the angels, pieced together the puzzle and "they remembered His words" (Luke 24:8).

Shortly after this Peter ran to the tomb, looked in and saw that the tomb was empty and only the linen napkins remained and he "went away to his home, marveling at that which had happened" (v. 12). Even though Peter had been taught directly by Jesus, he was astonished by the fact of the empty tomb. Peter, along with the other Jewish believers, found it exceedingly difficult to believe that the Messiah for whom they had prayed would have to suffer and die on a cross. And now He had risen.

The tomb was empty.

No man saw Jesus rise. Even His disciples were denied that privilege. They failed Him in the very difficult hours of the garden and so they were denied a share in the moment of His conquest, although they would share in the fruits of His conquest. The resurrection of Jesus Christ is not simply an event for faith. It is an event which took place in history. Faith is shallow indeed unless it is built on the bedrock of historical fact.

Annie Johnson Flint has written:
"He rose," saith the Tomb; "I was dark and drear,
And the sound of My Name wove a spell of fear;

But the Lord of Life in My depths hath lain
To break Death's power and rend his chain;
And a light streams forth from my open door,
For the Lord is risen; He dies no more."[2]

Many attempts have been made to deny the testimony of the empty tomb, and many ideas have been propounded to explain it.

One of these ideas is that the disciples stole the body. When the chief priests and the elders counseled together regarding the report from the guards who had been stationed at the tomb, they decided to bribe the soldiers and they were to tell people, "His disciples came by night and stole Him away while we were asleep" (Matt. 28:13). Our response to that theory is that the disciples were in no mood for that form of bravado. Instead they were full of fear and defeat. Little chance that they would have risked a battle with armed guards. There is no reason why the disciples would have wanted the body of Jesus. In addition, if the guards were sleeping, how would they know who stole the body of Jesus? Sleepers cannot identify those who rob their home at night.

Another idea is that the body was removed by Joseph of Arimathea.[3] Joseph Klausner maintained that the owner of the tomb had removed Jesus. Our response is that, there is no evidence to support this theory. After all, Joseph of Arimathea was a disciple too. If Klausner were right, the Sanhedrin could have saved the money that they spent on the bribes paid to the prison guards.

Still another thought is that the women went to the wrong tomb.[4] Kirsopp Lake said that the women, in their tearful, anxious state, ended up at the wrong tomb. Rather than going to the tomb of Joseph of Arimathea, they arrived at a vacant tomb. We must respond by saying that this was a private tomb and it would be difficult to miss, even in the

68

semi-darkness of early morning. If Jesus had been buried in a large memorial park with thousands of almost identical grave markings, I could be sympathetic with the theory. But isn't it interesting that Peter, John and the angels made the same mistake? They all went to the wrong tomb. It takes more faith to believe Lake's theory than it does to believe the teaching of Luke 24.

One other theory is that Christ never actually died. He swooned on the cross.[5] He swooned and was in a greatly weakened condition when placed in the tomb. The cool air revived Jesus in the succeeding days and He left the tomb. Our response takes the form of three questions: When in fact did He die then? If He were revived by the cool air, would He have sufficient strength to roll back the stone which undoubtedly weighed hundreds of pounds? And, even if He could move the stone, could He overpower the guards? It seems unlikely Christ "swooned" on the cross.

Jesus Christ Appeared to His Disciples

Jesus Christ, in His resurrected body, appeared to Mary Magdalene and to Peter, then to groups of apostles and on one occasion to more than 500. He appeared to James. He appeared to all the apostles. He appeared to the apostle Paul (1 Cor. 15:5-8).

If Jesus had risen from the tomb but had never appeared to anyone, it would require great faith to believe in His resurrection. Such is not the case. There is tremendous historical support for a resurrection. If there had not been a resurrection the radical critics would have to admit that Paul deceived the apostles about an actual appearance of Christ to him; they would have to admit that the apostles deceived Paul about Christ's appearances to them.

Critics have attempted to lessen the validity of the testimony of the post-resurrection appearances of Christ by offering alternate theories.

The believers saw Christ in a vision.[6] This hypothesis maintains that the believers saw their Lord in a spiritual way. They had a very graphic vision of Jesus, but He did not physically and literally appear to them.

My response is that visions may come to individuals or to small groups, but is it possible to believe that over 500 people would experience the same vision? Crowds do not receive visions. Furthermore, why would the visions stop? Why is it that the visions only occurred for six weeks?

The ascended Lord telegraphed back pictures of Himself to the minds of the apostles.[7] Canon Streeter, the author of this denial of post-resurrection theory, says that the telegraphing back of pictures was so vivid that the apostles believed they had actually seen Jesus.

The response of thoughtful Christians is that Jesus did not participate in a disillusion. This form of deception is contrary to all that we know about Jesus, who called Himself "the truth" (John 14:6).

The Lives of the Disciples Were Transformed

The book of Acts is the dramatic story of men whose lives were radically changed by an experience with the risen Christ. The feeble, faltering, faithless followers that we see cowering in the presence of enemies, sleeping in a garden, and hiding out for fear of their lives suddenly became a band of bold, courageous firebrands who were willing to die for their Lord.

The evidences of the empty tomb and of the post-resurrection appearances are impressive; but the greatest evidence of all is what happened to the disciples. Unless this band of men had actually encountered a resurrected Jesus

Christ who had conquered death and the tomb, their new behavior is difficult to explain.

Church tradition tells us that 10 of the 12 disciples died as martyrs. If Jesus had not risen, how much easier it would have been for them to return to their homes, families and occupations. But if they had met a resurrected Christ, the persecution and ultimate violent martyrdom is better understood.

What Does Christ's Resurrection Mean to Us?

If Christ had not been raised from the dead, then the backbone of Christianity would be defeated. First Corinthians 15:14 tells us that our preaching would be "in vain"; our faith would be placed in a mortal, finite Christ. However, because Christ did rise, we have a full and rich faith.

Christ's resurrection means that sin is defeated. Christ proved through the resurrection that He was the master over Satan, death and sin.

For generations men had wondered about the issue of sin: Was Satan the master? Would God finally yield to the power of the evil one?

The answer depended on the argument of ultimate accomplishment of Jesus Christ, sent of God to destroy the works of Satan. Through Christ our victory has already been won. The final issue is no longer a question. You and I will fight the battle of sin but Jesus has won the final victory. Because sin has been defeated, we are to acknowledge this victory and live in its light. First Corinthians 10:13 reminds us that temptation will come to everyone, but God, who is faithful, will show us how to be victorious. We can claim the victory of Christ.

Harry Ironside tells the story of a godly saint in Dundee, Scotland, who had been bedridden with a severe back

71

ailment for many years but had nevertheless maintained a positive, loving and gracious Christian spirit. Dr. Ironside mentions that when the angels passed over Dundee they probably stopped at this man's home for encouragement and refreshment!

On one occasion, Ironside visited with him and asked, "I'll bet you are never tempted by Satan. Sin must not be a problem for you."

The cripple responded immediately, "On the contrary. Satan often tempts me. When I see one of my old classmates go by the window with health and strength, Satan comes and says, 'Remember him? You were classmates. Today he has health and you are sickly. He is godless and you profess to be a Christian. God really doesn't care for you.'

"When I see someone drive by in a carriage, enjoying the out-of-doors, Satan comes to me and says, 'That man has nothing to do with God and look at him! You profess to know God and look at you!' "

Dr. Ironside asked, "Well, what do you do when this happens to you?"

"I take Satan by the hand and march him to Calvary and show him the nail-torn hands and feet of Jesus," replied the man. "I point to His side and His scarred brow and ask Satan, 'Doesn't He love me?' and Satan leaves me every-time."

Sin, then, is defeated. Calvary and the empty tomb prove that point conclusively.

Sin is very much alive today. You and I fight the battle at every turn. There are temptations of the flesh—to forget that our body is the temple of the Holy Spirit, to commit fornication or adultery, to fantasize impure actions in the mind. Television, movies and magazines bombard us with powerful temptations. To fight back, we need to claim the victory of the resurrected Christ. The plight of Satan is like that of a snake run over by an automobile. It is mortally wounded but may thrash about for hours in the death throes. Paul sums it up succinctly, "The sting of death is sin, and the power of sin is the law; but thanks be to God, who gives us the victory through our Lord Jesus Christ" (1 Cor. 15:56,57).

As a result of Christ's resurrection salvation is completed. The resurrection was the final act of God's saving drama. It was a fitting climax to His redemptive work on earth. The Resurrection was the divine act by which the Father gave the world a sign of His perfect satisfaction with the work of Christ. Jesus, His Son, had fulfilled the purpose of His coming. Jesus "was raised because of our justification" (Rom. 4:25). Justification is that powerful term that describes the fact that God treats me as innocent. I have been "made right." Justification springs from the grace of God (Rom. 3:24), is grounded on the fact of Christ's death and shed blood (Rom. 5:9), is proved by resurrection (Rom. 4:25), and is a divine provision which becomes ours by faith (Rom. 5:1).

Howard Butt discusses this reality and what it can mean to us. " 'Justification' is the word for *acceptance.* I accept you as you are because God accepts me as I am. 'Justification by faith' means you accept the gift of your acceptance. I do not have to reform, do better, improve, figure it out, straighten up, fly right, fulfill the law—or anything else—before I come to Christ. I come just as I am. In spiritual poverty, bankrupt before God. I take my acceptance as a beggar takes a free gift. All I need is to know my need. On the security of Christ's cross—a sacrifice for me complete, finished, perfected—I am totally, absolutely accepted. 'Justification'—just as if I'd never sinned. Golgotha's agony enables a Holy God to accept a sinful man like me and still be Holy Himself. The

Judge—the righteous Father—in the person of His Son—Himself takes the rap. Your faith accepts the gift. 'Being justified by faith we have peace with God' (Rom. 5:1 *KJV*). Then justification becomes contagious. 'Just as I am' I've been accepted; Now I can accept you *just as you are*. Peace with God and peace with each other come in a package: God makes me comfortable so I can make you comfortable."[8]

Nothing can be added to complete salvation. No amount of good works, rituals or religious observations can add one iota to the complete salvation that Jesus Christ provides through His death and resurrection. All I need to experience in salvation is a response of repentance because of my sin, and an act of faith in Jesus Christ who then becomes my Saviour. (See John 1:12; 3:16; Ephesians 2:8,9.)

Christ's resurrection is the guarantee of our resurrection (1 Cor. 15:20,51-54). Rumors and questions are dispelled; now believers can know that while death is certain, we shall be with Him!

At the time of Christ's second coming we shall meet Him to begin eternity together (1 Thess. 4:17). Or if our death precedes His return, we shall be absent from our earthly loved ones but "at home with the Lord" (2 Cor. 5:8). At the day of resurrection those who have died and are at home with the Lord shall be clothed in their resurrection bodies.

The resurrection of Jesus guarantees that not only shall we be with Him, but we shall be like Him. Jesus Christ will "transform the body of our humble state into conformity with the body of His glory, by the exertion of the power that He has even to subject all things to Himself" (Phil. 3:21).

Years ago, as a student at Moody Bible Institute, I became acquainted with an older gentleman who manned the desk in our dormitory. Ed knew and loved the Lord but served

Him with a broken body. Physically he was hurting. Some of his fingers were missing; he had a bad eye; he walked with a limp. Though unattractive to look at, Ed was a man who served his Lord very faithfully. In his free time he went to the Pacific Garden Mission and worked in the servicemen's center, leading scores to faith in Christ.

Someday, at the time of resurrection, Ed will receive a body like that of the Lord he served. I can envision the day when he stands in his resurrection body before the Lord whom he loved and hears those words of praise, "Well done, good and faithful servant" (see Matt. 25:21).

These bodies of ours wear out. Our teeth decay. Our hair drops out—some experience this more than others! Our limbs stiffen and our organs deteriorate. We finally give out. At the coming of Christ our salvation shall be complete—including body, soul and spirit. We shall be with Christ and we shall be like Christ. That glorious day is the hope of the resurrected people.

A little lad was gazing intently at the picture in the art store window: the store was displaying a notable picture of the crucifixion. A gentleman approached, stopped, and looked. The boy, seeing his interest, said, "That's Jesus." The man made no reply, and the lad continued, "Them's Roman soldiers." And, after a moment: "They killed Him."

"Where did you learn that?" asked the man.

"In the Mission Sunday School," was the reply.

The man turned and walked thoughtfully away. He had not gone far when he heard a youthful voice calling: "Say, Mister," and quickly the little street lad caught up with him. "Say, Mister," he repeated. "I wanted to tell you that He rose again."

That message which was nearly forgotten by the boy is the central message of the Christian faith. Without resurrection

75

there would be no Christians at all. The Christian church would never have begun and the Jesus movement would have fizzled out.

Christianity stands or falls with the truth of the Resurrection. The God Christ *is* risen. We are a people who serve a living Christ. We are a people with an incredible hope!

Additional Scriptures
for Study About the Resurrection
Psalm 16:10
Hosea 13:14
Matthew 16:21; 20:17-19; 28
Mark 9:9; 16
Luke 24
John 2:19-22; 20
Acts 1:3

Footnotes

1. *Evidence That Demands a Verdict* (Arrowhead Springs, California: Campus Crusade for Christ, Inc., 1972), p. 185.
2. Annie Johnson Flint quoted by J. Sidlow Baxter, *His Part and Ours* (Grand Rapids: Zondervan Publishing House, 1960), p. 92.
3. Wilbur M. Smith, *Therefore Stand* (Boston: W.A. Wilde Co., 1945), pp. 378-381.
4. Smith, *Therefore Stand*, pp. 381,382.
5. Smith, *Therefore Stand*, p. 383.
6. Smith, *Therefore Stand*, pp. 393-397.
7. Smith, *Therefore Stand*, pp. 397,398.
8. Howard Butt, *The Velvet Covered Brick* (New York: Harper & Row Publishers, 1973), p. 34.

6. What Has Christ Been Doing for 1900 Years?

"I believe in …Jesus Christ…(who) ascended into heaven, and sitteth on the right hand of God the Father Almighty."

After 33 years of earthly life, Jesus Christ returned to the heavenly Father. He spent 30 of these years in relative obscurity, three in public ministry. I have already noted the importance of His birth, His death and His resurrection: He came into this world supernaturally, He died for our sins and He was resurrected for our justification.

After His post-resurrection appearances, Jesus ascended to the Father. As the disciples gazed intently into the sky, watching their Lord disappear, two angels appeared and said, "Men of Galilee, why do you stand looking into the sky? This Jesus, who has been taken up from you into heaven, will come in just the same way as you have watched Him go into heaven" (Acts 1:11).

The angels said Christ would return. We do not know the date of His second coming. It could be at any moment. The responsibility of the church until He returns is to be serving faithfully, and be healthy, active and ready to meet Him.

The Ascended Christ

Only recently I ran across a double ascension theory put forth by Lewis Sperry Chafer, and I find it quite convincing. I commend the theory to you as a helpful explanation of the seemingly conflicting teachings (John 20 and Luke 24) regarding the return of Christ to heaven.

Chafer divides Christ's upward movements into two events: the ascension on resurrection morning and the final ascension after 40 days. He notes that John 20:17 forbids Mary from touching Him, and yet Luke 24:38-40 shows Jesus offering His body to the disciples to be touched. "The implication is clear that, since He could not be touched in the morning and yet could be 'handled' at evening of the same day, He had ascended during the day."[1]

The purpose of Christ's first ascension was to appear at once in heaven, in triumph, to finish the work of redemption. It is the picture of the high priest entering the holy of holies (Heb. 9:11,12). The purpose of His second ascension was to mark the visible, final departure from earth to heaven and His rightful place at His Father's throne (Rom. 8:34).

Jesus is no longer a spirit. "It is the Man in the glory . . . He is there corporeally in the body of His glory."[2] Jesus is at the right hand of the Father in His resurrected body. When He came to earth He surrendered omnipresence (that is, being present everywhere at once).

You may recall that Jesus told His disciples, "It is to your advantage that I go away; for if I do not go away, the Helper shall not come to you; but if I go, I will send Him to you"

(John 16:7). One of the reasons Jesus said this was that, as the incarnate God, it wasn't possible for Him to be two places at once. Such a limitation is not true of the Holy Spirit. He can indwell all believers at once. Jesus chose to empty Himself of His omnipresence and as such continues in His resurrected body.

The Present Work of Christ

The present work of Christ, known as "His Session," is twofold: as High Priest and as Head of the Church.

Jesus is the High Priest. Hebrews 8:1-3 says, "We have such a high priest, who has taken His seat at the right hand of the throne of the Majesty in the heavens, a minister in the sanctuary, and in the true tabernacle, which the Lord pitched, not man. For every high priest is appointed to offer both gifts and sacrifices; hence it is necessary that this high priest also have something to offer." Earlier in the book of Hebrews Jesus is called the "Apostle" and the "High Priest of our confession" (Heb. 3:1). As the High Priest He fulfills three functions: He is *mediator* and as such seeks to reconcile God and sinful man; He is *intercessor* and as such pleads with God to keep the believer from sin; and He is the *advocate* and as such He pleads with God when the believer sins.

First, Jesus, the High Priest, as mediator is the only work of the exalted Christ that reaches out to the world as a whole, not only to believers. Paul wrote to Timothy about this function of Jesus Christ: "That God is on one side and all the people on the other side, and Christ Jesus, himself man, is between them to bring them together, by giving his life for all mankind" (1 Tim. 2:5,6, *TLB*).

The purpose of Christ's mediation is clearly that of redemption. By definition, to mediate means to intervene in order to bring about a reconciliation. The assumption is that the mediator is an equal friend of both parties. The same concept carries over into international law, where one power will stand between two other powers to arrange a settling of their differences.

Recently there have been some much publicized salary conflicts between major league baseball players and the club owners. An arbitrator has been brought in to decide the issue. The goal in each instance is a peaceable solution. Jesus, the mediator, stands between God the Father and sinful mankind to bring about a reconciliation.

The concept of mediation has been frequently confused during the last 1900 years of church history. Some have taught that long-dead saints have an inside track to God and we must, therefore, pray to them and through them. For example, Mary, the Mother of Christ, is one through whom many have prayed, feeling that certainly Jesus would be more sympathetic to His mother than to one of us. If pushed to its logical conclusion this means that Mary is more compassionate than Jesus because she always listens whereas Jesus does not. This, of course, is blasphemous. It was once fashionable for people to have a metallic "Christopher figure" on the dashboard of their car, as if safety on the highway might be secured by a saint who interceded on behalf of travelers.

The entire mediatorial system with its many saints is founded upon human logic and not upon the teaching of Scripture, which claims there is only "one mediator between God and man" (see 1 Tim. 2:5).

During a strike of the Masons' Union in Los Angeles, our church learned a fresh appreciation for the mediator's role. For nine weeks our church building project stood almost silent without a bricklayer on the job. It was frustrating to all of us, who were anxious for our new church facility to be completed. An arbitrator was brought in to reconcile the differences between the unions and management. Soon, our building project was nearing completion, thanks in part to the work of the arbitrator who served as mediator. Of greater importance both here and into eternity is the ministry of the ascended Christ, who mediates between God and sinful man to provide for our salvation.

The second function of Jesus as High Priest is as intercessor. To intercede is to act between parties with a view to reconcile their differences. This concept is very similar to that of mediation. The distinction is that intercession is prayer on behalf of the *believer* only.

Christ, Himself, prayed for believers while on earth. "I ask on their behalf; I do not ask on behalf of the world, but of those whom Thou hast given Me; for they are Thine" (John 17:9). At present Jesus is in heaven to "appear in the presence of God for us" (Heb. 9:24). The Saviour knows our weaknesses; He knows Satan's power and the many temptations we face, and He prays for us (see Heb. 4:14-16). Jesus, during His 33 years of earthly life, experienced all the types of temptations and tests we face today. As such He sympathizes with us and prays to the Father on our behalf. His ministry is unending and effectual (see Heb. 7:25).

Years ago I heard a sermon in which the preacher related this story. Author C.I. Scofield was depressed and downcast one morning. It was as if a heavy cloud were just overhead—but suddenly it lifted. A friend of his came by. "You must have prayed for me today," said Scofield.

"No," said the friend, "but I know your great High Priest and intercessor, Jesus Christ, and He talked to the Father about you."

A.B. Simpson has written that Jesus our intercessor

separates from our prayer all that is imperfect, ignorant and wrong, and presents the rest, with the incense of the great High Priest, before the throne on high; and our prayer is heard, accepted and answered in His name."

Third, Jesus, the High Priest is an advocate. An advocate pleads the cause of another, as before a tribunal or judicial court. The High Priest in heaven prays for us before we sin (intercession), but he also pleads for us when we sin (advocacy). The Scripture says: "My little children, I am writing these things to you that you may not sin. And if anyone sins, we have an Advocate with the Father, Jesus Christ the righteous; and He Himself is the propitiation for our sins; and not for ours only, but also for those of the whole world" (1 John 2:1,2).

The fact of Jesus Christ pleading our case before God the Father is not dependent upon our repentance or confession. The moment we sin our advocate reminds the Father of His blood which was shed for us. What may be a secret sin on earth is an open scandal in heaven. It can't be treated lightly. By grace we are kept saved.

Picture, if you will, a courtroom scene. God the Father is the judge. Dan Baumann is the defendant, Satan is the accuser (according to Rev. 12:10, he is the consistent pest who "day and night" accuses the brethren but who will one day be cast into hell). The defense attorney is Jesus Christ. Satan comes before God the judge and says, "I have recently visited Whittier and observed one of your children, Dan Baumann. Let me assure you that he has no perfect record. I have caught him on more than one occasion becoming impatient with his children, sharp with his wife and proud (for whatever reasons I have not been able to discover) of some of his sermons. According to your inerrant Bible, oh Judge, the wages of sin is death (see Rom. 6:23) and upon such good authority I maintain that Dan Baumann is a sinner and deserves eternal punishment. I rest my case."

Jesus Christ, the defense attorney, is called to the floor. God the Judge asks, "Have you heard the testimony brought against your defendant? And what do you have to say on his behalf?"

Jesus once again recounts the facts of Calvary, how He became sin, taking upon Himself the penalty for the sins of the world. He indicates His scarred hands and feet and points to His side.

The Judge's reply? "Case dismissed!"

For the eternal encouragement of the Christian church, it is to be noted that Jesus has not lost a case in over 1900 years. In ourselves we are guilty and hell deserving, but in Christ we are innocent. The advocacy of Jesus Christ reminds us that it is not necessary to be saved again, again and again. As one person put it, "There is a new name written down in glory—and it is not in pencil." We are indelibly and eternally the children of God. Thanks to the present work of Christ, our advocate.

Jesus is the Head of the Church. The graphic statement regarding the church and its ministry is found in the book of Ephesians. Paul, in writing to the church at Ephesus, says that God the Father raised Christ "from the dead, and seated Him at His right hand in the heavenly places, far above all rule and authority and power and dominion, and every name that is named, not only in this age, but also in the one to come. And He put all things in subjection under His feet, and gave Him as head over all things to the church, which is His body, the fulness of Him who fills all in all" (Eph. 1:20-23). In another one of his letters, Paul refers to Christ as "head of the body, the church" (Col. 1:18).

Two roles of Jesus as head of the Church deserve

attention. First, Jesus is the bestower of gifts. The ascended and exalted Christ gives gifts to the Church. Recently much has been written about the gifts of the spirit, commonly called the charismata, or spiritual or grace gifts. Not only is the Holy Spirit the dispenser of gifts (see 1 Cor. 12:7), but Christ is spoken of as the giver of gifts also (see Eph. 4:7). If we add together the spiritual gifts from Romans 12:6-8, 1 Corinthians 12:4-11 and Ephesians 4:7-13, we have approximately 19 separate gifts. Jesus Christ and the Holy Spirit in concert distribute these gifts sovereignly to all Christians.

Every Christian is gifted (see 1 Cor. 12:7), and these gifts are sovereignly distributed (1 Cor. 12:11); that is to say, the possession of gifts isn't dependent upon our choice but God's will. We are given these gifts to equip the saints for the work of ministry, to build up the body of Christ and to bring individuals to maturity. (See Eph. 4:12,13,15.)

The church I pastor has a slogan which says that we are a church with over 900 ministers. We take this concept from Ephesians 4. The pastoral staff exists to equip all the members of the church to serve as ministers. This distinction is often forgotten by the modern church. Pastors and fulltime Christian workers are called ministers whereas the Bible teaches that all God's people are ministers. One day an outsider saw our slogan in the yellow pages and said, "If you have over 900 ministers, you must have thousands of laymen!!"

Included in the 19 gifts are evangelism, teaching, mercy, liberality, shepherding, and the like. Every congregation will generally have these same gifts represented in its membership.

We can be grateful that the present work of Christ includes the gifting of individuals for the purpose of bringing the church to maturity. I believe that one of the major tasks of the local church is to so teach the biblical statements regarding spiritual gifts that congregations will be informed regarding the great diversity of Christ's gifts and also that individuals will begin to identify their gifts and use them for the glory of God and the good of the local church.

I am further convinced that the identification of spiritual gifts is a task all of us must assume. It is generally easier for someone else to define my gifts than for me to do so.

The reason for this is quite simple. Gifts are given for the health of the members of the church. That is to say that the very same individuals who have been helped can help many individuals discover what my gifts are for the ministry. I encourage you, therefore, to help others around you identify their gifts so they can begin to serve Christ independently as a fulfilled gifted Christian.

As head of the church Jesus is also the builder of our eternal home. One day Jesus took the discouraged band of apostles aside and told them He would be returning to the Father. In the midst of that discourse, recorded in John 14, He told them He was going to prepare a place for them. We can only begin to imagine what it is that our Lord is creating for us. In the place of honor at the right hand of the Father, He is building chairman, architect, and contractor of that "housing development" in glory.

Here on earth life can be transitory. Americans are constantly on the move. Our church directory has to be updated almost every single week, and our people are no different from anybody else. Businesses transfer their employees, individuals get tired of one location and move to another. Some can no longer afford the high taxes in one community and move to another. Mobility is our middle name.

There are those who cannot afford to purchase a home.

Inflation has so skyrocketed real estate costs that the purchase of an average home requires monthly payments of $400-$500. As a result, many can't ever imagine living in a lovely home in a beautiful community, simply because the cost is exorbitant.

Recently two of the richest men in the world died—Howard Hughes and John Paul Getty. They were worth billions of dollars and yet neither appeared to enjoy life. With all their wealth, existence seemed rather grim. From all outside appearances neither knew Jesus Christ as Saviour. At the time of their deaths they left all their riches. What a contrast this is to the child of God who in death goes home to his riches!

The Scriptures tell us that there are "many dwelling places" (John 14:2). There will be enough for all. I have to believe that Solomon's temple with its extravagant use of gold even to the floors will be a shed in comparison to the mansions our Lord is preparing for His blood-purchased church. It is the very nature of God to go beyond our farthest imagination in the lavish display of His grace. While we are pilgrims on this earth we may enjoy a few luxuries but our greatest glory and fondest hope is reserved at the presence of the Father in heaven. All those in Christ have the hope that our Lord is for us "the way, the truth and the life" (John 14:6).

Jesus ascended to the right hand of the Father approximately in A.D. 29. His return could be any time. In the interim Christ, the High Priest, ministers on behalf of His church.

> I know that my Redeemer lives,
> What comfort this sweet sentence gives!
> He lives, He lives who once was dead,
> He lives, my ever-living Head.

He lives. He reigns in yonder skies,
He lives, and I from death shall rise.
He lives, my mansion to prepare,
He lives, to bring me safely there.
He lives, and will return in power,
He lives, He comes, O golden hour!
He lives, all glory to His Name,
He lives, my Jesus, still the same!
O the sweet joy this sentence gives,—
"I know that my Redeemer lives!"[3]

Additional Scriptures
for Study About the Risen Christ as Intercessor

Psalm 68:18
Mark 16:19
Luke 24:51
John 6:62; 20:17
Acts 1:9
Hebrews 4:14,15
1 Peter 3:22

Footnotes

1. Lewis Sperry Chafer, *Systematic Theology,* vol. 5 (Wheaton, Illinois: Van Kampen Press, 1950), p. 263.
2. E. Schuyler English, *Things Surely to Be Believed,* vol. 1 (Wheaton, Illinois: Van Kampen Press, 1946), p. 105.
3. J. Sidlow Baxter, *His Part and Ours* (Grand Rapids: Zondervan Publishing House, 1960) p. 99.

7. Watch What You Do— It Could Come Back to Haunt You!

"I believe in Jesus Christ...(who) shall come to judge the quick and the dead."

A few years ago I joined the Minneapolis Police Department's "Ride Along" program for citizens. I arrived about 7:30 P.M. at the downtown police station, signed a waiver, was introduced to two young good-looking policemen and joined them in their unmarked car. It was a night I will never forget. Following some routine police situations—speeding cars, a couple of domestic situations (husband and wife battles), we received a call about midnight announcing that four men had just fled the scene of a tavern robbery.

Immediately my two new friends from the police department moved into action. They put their hats on, turned on their red light and sped to an intersection that was bound to

89

intercept the fleeing robbers. Sure enough, they were along in a matter of seconds. The chase with red light flashing and tires squealing took us quickly through the downtown section, across railroad tracks, over a bridge and finally to a lonely, deserted side street where "we" pulled them to a curb.

The two policemen got out of the car with guns drawn. They took the suspects' two shotguns, placed them in the rear seat of the police car and began to frisk the four men. In the process three of them jumped the one policeman, leaving one robber and one policeman on the sidelines. The three men worked over the policeman, two holding him and the other hitting him across the face.

In a flash of almost superman-like strength, the policeman broke loose from their grip, hit one across the jaw and sent him sprawling across the hood of their car, took the second and flipped him over his shoulders, and put a hammerlock on the third of his assailants while the second policeman lined them against the robbers' car and demanded they raise their hands skyward. The four men were handcuffed and additional police cars were summoned to transport them to the city jail. They were fingerprinted and booked for robbery, speeding, resisting arrest, assault and battery.

At 4:00 A.M. I left the city jail, returning home with a fresh appreciation for the problem of maintaining law and order in contemporary society. The interesting thing to me is that everybody involved in this case will some day stand before Jesus, the righteous judge. The four robbers, the two valiant policemen, the booking officer at the jail, the judge before whom they would soon appear in court, and one wide-eyed seminary professor named Dan Baumann. The teaching of Scripture is clear: Christians and non-Christians alike must give account of their life in the future. To be sure the judgments differ in character, but no one can escape the fact of judgment.

This doctrine of judgment is not popular. Many theologians and preachers of a more liberal tendency dismiss the concept of future judgment. Yes, the judgment of Christ is not a popular doctrine; but on the other hand, the love of Christ is an exceedingly popular doctrine. Nearly everyone rallies to a theology of love and compassion, but the appeal significantly lessens when you talk of Christ as judge. Why? It simply does not fit the image of God maintained by many.

Opponents of the doctrine of judgment do not view God as a God of wrath, but as a God of love. However, because God is God and not man, divine love transcends human love and divine wrath transcends human wrath. It is vital that Christian theologians include the teaching of judgment because of its biblical support. We must accept the whole counsel of God—both for love and for justice.

God's Program of Judgment

Jesus entered our world with a divine mission. When the time was ripe, He died on the cross as a ransom for many and returned to heaven, following His resurrection, to be glorified. At some unknown time in the future He will return. Included in the events of the end times will be a program of judgment. Two judgments stand out—the general judgment and the judgment of believers. Let's look at the first.

Matthew 25:31-46 establishes God's principles of general judgment. This text is a reference more to the standards and process of judgment than to an event per se. Here we see that all the people of the world are divided into two groups: Sheep—a biblical metaphor for believers (See Ps. 23:1 and Isa. 53:6), and goats—a biblical metaphor for the ungodly.

91

Professor John Broadus tells of an experience he once had: "The morning after reaching Palestine, when setting out . . . across the plain of Sharon, we saw a shepherd leading forth a flock of white sheep and black goats, all mingled as they followed him. Presently he turned aside into a little green valley, and stood facing the flock. When a sheep came up, he tapped it with his long staff on the right side of the head, and it quickly moved off to his right; a goat he tapped on the other side, and it went to his left. Thus the Saviour's image presented itself exactly before our eyes."[1]

In Matthew 25:35,36 we read that the basis for this general judgment is works. Those who pass the test have fed the hungry, given drink to the thirsty, invited strangers into their home, clothed the naked, attended to the sick, and visited the imprisoned. How is it that an eternal destiny of punishment or life (Matt. 25:46) is based upon works? How do you square this teaching with the teaching of Ephesians 2:8,9, where we are told that "You have been saved through faith; and that not of yourselves, it is the gift of God; not as a result of works, that no one should boast."

In part the answer is to be found in a comparison of Scripture with Scripture. Man is saved by faith, but according to the book of James, faith that is real shows itself in works. "Faith, if it has no works, is dead, being by itself" (Jas. 2:17). Matthew 25 is passing judgment on the fruits of faith rather than on faith itself. The result of this judgment is an eternal division of mankind, either into "eternal punishment" or "eternal life" (Matt. 25:46).

In Revelation 20:11-15, we have the event of the general judgment which is called the "Great White Throne" judgment. Following the millenium reign of Jesus Christ upon this earth at the conclusion of human history, there will be this final vindication of God's righteousness. There, the division of all mankind will be accomplished. There is hell for the unbeliever (i.e. the lake of fire—Rev. 20:15), or there is eternal life in the presence of God for those whose name is "written in the book of life." This will be a visual demonstration of the eternal victory of Jesus Christ in the salvation of those who have faith in Him and the punishment and destruction of those who reject Him.

First Corinthians 3:10-15 speaks of the judgment of believers. This, too, is a future event, and the time setting is not easy to determine. The judgment probably occurs following the Great White Throne Judgment at the completion of God's program for His people. Although the time setting is somewhat difficult and open to differing interpretations, the truth of that judgment is much easier to establish. The judgment of believers does not deal with sin or with the question of salvation, it deals instead with faithfulness and rewards.

Some Christians will have the painful exposure of a wasted life. Nothing of their life will remain. "Wood, hay and straw" (v. 12) of their life will be destroyed by the fire of Christ's test. At that point they will be empty-handed. If there are any tears in heaven, it could be assumed that it will occur at that time. The text graphically says, "If any man's work is burned up, he shall suffer loss; but he himself shall be saved, yet so as through fire" (v. 15). An unknown author has penned lines of challenge revealing that potential scene:

When I stand at the judgment seat of Christ
And He shows me His plan for me,
The plan of my life as it might have been
Had He had His way, and I see
How I blocked Him here, and I checked Him there,
And I would not yield my will,
Will there be grief in my Saviour's eyes,

93

Grief, though He loves me still?
   He would have made me rich, and I stand there poor,
   Stripped of all but His grace,
   While memory runs like a hunted thing
   Down the paths I cannot retrace.
Then my desolate heart will well-nigh break
With the tears that I cannot shed;
I shall cover my face with my empty hands,
I shall bow my uncrowned head.
   Lord, of the years that are left to me,
   I give them to Thy hand:
   Take me and break me, mould me to
   The pattern Thou hast planned.[2]

On the other hand, many Christians will receive trophies of faithful ministry in Jesus' name. They will have built their life upon a foundation of "gold, silver, precious stones" (v. 12) which pass the fire test of Christ's judgment. This public recognition of faithfulness will isolate individuals who may have received nothing of earlier applause and recognition. I visualize a time of triumph for preschool Sunday School teachers who change diapers of screaming children, gather toys and, for hours, hold little ones in their arms and tell them that God is love. I visualize a time of triumph for parents who prayed and modeled and geared their wayward children into paths of useful Christian living. I visualize a time of triumph for pastors who labored in small, rural churches devoid of large numbers, publicity and denominational records; for men who visited the sick, comforted the grief-ridden, studied late into the night for years in order to lead in small Sunday School classes, midweek prayer services and sparsely-attended morning and evening worship services.

I see a time of triumph for missionaries who lived in a

primitive setting, labored with the difficult dialect of a Philippine tribe to decipher the language and, after a score of years, completed a handwritten New Testament in the language of that people. I anticipate a time of triumph for missionaries who at the end of their life could not marshal thousands of converts to testify to their faithfulness, but who left behind them perhaps no more than a dozen trophies of grace, a Bible in the hands of the people and a record of heroism and faith.

The time of believers' judgment will give recognition to such unheralded acts as the intercessory prayer of trusting Christians, letters of encouragement sent by caring believers and acts of tenderness expressed in the privacy of the home.

Lest We Forget!

Three important principles or truths undergird God's program of judgment through Jesus Christ.

Judgment is certain. Hebrews 9:27 says, "Inasmuch as it is appointed for men to die once, and after this comes judgment." Man may flaunt God in this world but he must ultimately face Him in the next. This judgment for believers and unbelievers alike is as certain as death and taxes.

The truth of this coming judgment is sometimes acknowledged in the strangest ways, in the most unusual settings. Don Rickles, the comedian with the caustic tongue, appeared on Johnny Carson's "Tonight Show" and during his routine made the comment, "If I am not telling the truth, may I be struck with paralysis," and then acted as if he had had a stroke. The audience laughed nervously. I had an uneasy feeling that many of them realized that although paralysis may not be the method of God's judgment, the sentiment is understood in the hearts of men. The way of truth will be vindicated and the way of untruth must be punished. Man cannot forever fly in the face of righteousness without having to finally give an answer to God. The rope may be long, but it has an end to it.

An irreligious farmer in one of the western states wrote a letter to his local newspaper. "Sir: I have been trying an experiment with a field of mine. I have plowed on Sunday, planted on Sunday, cultivated on Sunday, reaped on Sunday and hauled the crops into my barn on Sunday. And do you know the result? I have more bushels to the acre in that field than any of my neighbors have had this October." He undoubtedly expected some applause of recognition by the editor, but instead the editor simply added one line of comment: "God doesn't always settle His accounts in October."

Judgment will be righteous. Romans 2:5 speaks of the righteous judgment of God. No court of law in our country is immune from mistakes. On occasion, though certainly infrequently, the innocent are punished and the guilty are released. By and large we may rest in the wisdom and the honesty of the law courts of our land.

But it is a well-known fact of history that not every judgment is correct. In fact, occasionally problems confuse justice in the twentieth century. God's judgment, we can be assured, will be free from mistake, prejudice, or graft. The right thing will occur.

Most of the decisions coming from the Supreme Court of our land represent a split vote. For example, a few years back the law section article in *Time* magazine spoke of a "new 5-4 majority," the reference to the fact that the Supreme Court had moved from the liberalism of the Warren Supreme Court to the more conservative Burger Supreme Court, because of two conservative judges appointed by then-president Richard Nixon. By absolute standards the possibility of a 5-4 right judgment seemed strange indeed. Truth ought always to be 9-0. When God makes His judgments through Jesus Christ, you may rest assured that the innocent will be vindicated and the guilty will be judged.

Judgment is personal. Romans 14:10 reminds us that "we shall all stand before the judgment-seat of God" and then adds in verse 12, "each one of us shall give account of himself to God." There will be no opportunity for scapegoats.

Judgment is supremely personal. Paul Rees, the gifted evangelical expositor, once wrote, "Basically, it is a trait of our human sinfulness: we must put the blame on shoulders other than our own. Psychologically it is a strongly American trait. Our breezy buoyant, boundlessly self-confident manner suddenly flips when it is frustrated. When things go collectively wrong, we look frantically for a villain. The villain of the piece may be anyone—from an 'Al' Capone to an occupant of the White House. Scapegoat-hunting is much easier than soul-searching. This, partly, is because it leaves our pride and impenitence intact."[3]

There is a tendency for all of us to look for scapegoats, to "pass the buck." After Adam sinned, he blamed the woman. When God approached the woman, she blamed the serpent. None of us likes to stand and be judged on his own merit. Exodus 32 records one of the strangest stories in all of Scripture. Aaron, while Moses was in the mountain receiving the Ten Commandments, made a calf of gold. When Moses asked him about this act of disobedience he replied to the effect that people had given him gold. "I threw it into the fire, and out came this calf!" (Exod. 32:24). Sounds a little farfetched, if you ask me!

For the unbeliever, judgment is a fearful thing. Repentance must be made during the day of grace—today is the day of salvation. The best way to prepare for the Great White Throne Judgment is to place faith in Jesus Christ as personal Saviour, to once and for all settle the sin problem.

For the believer there is no fear. First Thessalonians 5:9 says, "For God has not destined us for wrath, but for obtaining salvation through our Lord Jesus Christ."

"There is no fear in love; but perfect love casts out fear, because fear involves punishment, and the one who fears is not perfected in love" (1 John 4:18). Christians may or may not receive rewards at their judgment, but their salvation is as certain as the promises of God's Word.

Additional Scriptures
for Study About Christ, the Judge
Matthew 25:31-46
John 5:22,23
Acts 10:42; 17:30,31
Romans 2:14-16
1 Corinthians 4:5
2 Timothy 4:1,2

Footnotes

1. John Broadus. Source Unknown.
2. *Anchor*, Sept. 1976, Vol 1, No. 7. A Ministry of the Crew of the Good Ship Grace, Inc. Haven of Rest Broadcast.
3. Paul S. Rees, *The World Vision Magazine*, November, 1962.

8. The Mysterious Third Person of the Trinity

"I believe in the Holy Ghost."

A young people's newspaper carried the following poem written by a fourth grader:

> I love God.
>> Do you?
> I believe in Jesus.
>> Do you?
> The Holy Spirit is in me.
>> Is it in you?

The sentiment expressed by this young lady is a model for all believers. She loves God, the Father. She believes in Jesus, His Son, and she is indwelt by God the Holy Spirit. She has captured a basic teaching of the Word of God regarding the Trinity. We can hardly blame her for the one theological confusion in her poem—referring to the Holy

Spirit as "it." The Holy Spirit is a *person.* As such we do not refer to the Holy Spirit as "it," but "He."

Children are not the only ones who may have difficulty understanding and believing in the Holy Spirit as a person. Vast numbers of adult believers have the same difficulty. The biblical doctrine of God is helped along in its appeal to our understanding by the fact that we have a frame of reference in which to place it; namely human fatherhood. This image, when it is applied to God, is concrete, familiar and, for most folks, attractive. Although we may not understand the profound inner relationship between the Father and the Son, we do find a meaningful analogy in the human.

For some, the doctrine of the Holy Spirit is irrelevant. I listened one evening to a guest surgeon discuss a sermon he had heard his pastor preach on the Holy Spirit. It was obvious that the doctor felt it was a waste of time. After all, he said, this teaching "has nothing to do with us." There are always those who shy away from the doctrine of the Holy Spirit because they have a fear of the mysterious. To talk about the Holy Ghost reminds people of creatures wearing white sheets running around on October 31 trying to scare little children. The whole thing is really quite spooky.

It is helpful to remember that the most significant thing about us and our friends is spiritual. The greatest realities of life are not always tangible and physical. Take personality— it is spiritual. When a coroner examines a corpse, he finds everything physical that was there before the person died. But the human spirit, the most meaningful reality about that individual, is not there. So it is the spirit that makes possible our life and our experience of those things of greatest value and meaning. If you transfer this thought to God, it may help you to understand the personal intimacy with which

God as the Holy Spirit seeks communion with your spirit.

Scripturally, we discover that the Holy Spirit is eternal and equal with the Father and the Son. The doctrine of the Holy Spirit must be seen as it unfolds in Scriptures in three very distinct periods of history: the Old Testament period, the New Testament until Pentecost, and Pentecost and following.

The Old Testament Period

Documentation of the Holy Spirit's work begins with creation. "In the beginning God created the heavens and the earth. And the earth was formless and void, and darkness was over the surface of the deep; and the Spirit of God was moving over the surface of the waters" (Gen. 1:1,2). The Holy Spirit, in concert with God the Father and God the Son, brought our universe into being, a present and active agent of the creation, "Let *us* make . . ." (Gen. 1:26).

Through the remainder of the Old Testament, the Holy Spirit works to enable people to carry out certain tasks. He does not indwell all believers, nor does He stay with any believer throughout his whole life. He comes upon individuals for special missions only. He comes and He goes according to the will of God.

Five separate incidents will bear out this reality:

1. The Holy Spirit was taken from Moses and given to the 70 elders. "Then the Lord came down in the cloud and spoke to him; and He took of the Spirit who was upon him and placed Him upon the seventy elders. And it came about that when the Spirit rested upon them, they prophesied. But they did not do it again" (Num. 11:25).

2. In Numbers 24:2, we read that the Spirit came upon Balaam and enabled him to prophesy to the people of Israel.

3. On another occasion the Spirit of God came upon

101

Samson, giving him the special ability to rip a lion in pieces with his bare hands (Judg. 14:6).

4. Still another time, Samuel told Saul that the Spirit of God would come upon him in mighty fashion. The prophecy is fulfilled in the words recorded in 1 Samuel 10:10, "When they came to the hill there, behold, a group of prophets met him; and the Spirit of God came upon him mightily, so that he prophesied among them."

5. Some time later the Spirit of the Lord departed from Saul.

The pattern visible in these five events is unbroken: During the Old Testament period, the Holy Spirit was given to enable men to serve God. When the task had been completed or there was disobedience on the part of the believer or the purposes of God were modified, the Spirit of God was taken from the individual. This does not imply that salvation was taken, but simply that the provision of the Holy Spirit for special ministries was removed.

The New Testament Period Prior to Pentecost

Practically speaking, New Testament times begin with the events leading to the supernatural birth of Jesus Christ. The miraculous conception of Mary was due to the ministry of the third member of the Trinity, the Holy Spirit (Luke 1:35). At the age of 30, Jesus left the obscurity of Nazareth and the carpenter shop to begin three years of public ministry.

The first act in His public ministry was His baptism by John the Baptist in the River Jordan. Following this act of identification with mankind, as Jesus came up out of the baptismal waters, the heavens opened and "He saw the Spirit of God descending as a dove, and coming upon Him, and behold, a voice out of the heavens, saying, 'This is My beloved Son, in whom I am well-pleased' " (Matt. 3:16,17).

In this instance we see the Holy Spirit as a dove adding His blessing, delegating power upon Jesus.

During the entire public ministry of Jesus, the Holy Spirit was actively involved. He came to Jesus at His baptism and stayed until Jesus ascended to the Father. The only time the Holy Spirit possibly may have left Jesus was during the crucifixion, when Jesus became sin for us, when the Saviour cried out, "My God, My God, why hast Thou forsaken Me?" (Matt. 27:46).

Almost immediately after the baptism of Jesus, the Holy Spirit led the Saviour into the wilderness where He was to experience 40 days of fasting followed by the three-fold temptation by the devil. After Jesus' complete triumph over Satan we read that "Jesus returned . . . in the power of the Spirit" (Luke 4:14).

During the earthly life of Christ, the entire period prior to Pentecost, very little is said about the relationship of the Holy Spirit to the disciples or to other believers. It seems however, that the Holy Spirit was available as men asked for Him. Luke 11:13 reads, "How much more shall your heavenly Father give the Holy Spirit to those who ask Him?"

As far as the record goes, no one ever asked. The offer had been made, but seemingly no one took advantage of this promise. Near the end of the earthly ministry of Jesus the promise of the Holy Spirit was given in John 15:26. "When the Helper comes, whom I will send to you from the Father, that is the Spirit of truth, who proceeds from the Father, He will bear witness of Me." The promise is restated at the Master's ascension, when He gave those well-known last words recorded in Acts 1:8, "But you shall receive power when the Holy Spirit has come upon you; and you shall be My witnesses both in Jerusalem, and in all Judea and Samaria, and even to the remotest part of the earth."

Pentecost: Key to the Present and Future

On the day of Pentecost the Holy Spirit came upon the church in fulfillment of Christ's last prophecy. A group of 120 had returned to Jerusalem from the Mount of Olives to spend time in prayer in the Upper Room. They devoted themselves to prayer, the selection of a replacement for Judas, and anticipation of the coming of the Holy Spirit. Such a vivid account is made of that day's events! "There came from heaven a noise like a violent, rushing wind, and it filled the whole house where they were sitting. And there appeared to them tongues as of fire distributing themselves, and they rested on each one of them. And they were all filled with the Holy Spirit and began to speak with other tongues, as the Spirit was giving them utterance" (Acts 2:2-4).

The coming of the Spirit initiated a new period of God's work. Not only was the modern missionary movement initiated in the supernatural sharing of the gospel in the languages of the people (Acts 2:2,4,6,8), but a provision was made for empowering believers through the indwelling omnipresent Holy Spirit.

From Pentecost until the present the Holy Spirit has been active in the world in a variety of ways.

The Holy Spirit converts new believers. John 16:8-11 tells us of this work of conviction concerning sin and righteousness and judgment. The work of the Holy Spirit in conviction is something that occurs prior to conversion. People are broken before God under the convincing, convicting power of the Holy Spirit.

Because I was only a boy of eight when I encountered Christ, I do not have clear memories of that conviction. During the years of my own ministry, however, I have met scores of people who have related their struggle as the Spirit of God came to them. For some it is a time characterized by sleepless nights, agonizing days, lashing out at friends and finally a submission to God. For others it is a quiet, certain struggle in the sanctuary of the soul, culminating in a yielding to the grace of God.

The Holy Spirit regenerates believers. When we become a Christian, God the Father comes to us in grace, revealing the finished work of Christ on our behalf; but it is the Holy Spirit who regenerates us, who makes us new. In John 3:6 we read, "That which is born of the flesh is flesh; and that which is born of the Spirit is spirit." Nicodemus found his whole conversation with Jesus to be incredible. Jesus told him he must be born again and all that the learned teacher of the Jews could think of was a return visit to the womb. To him it was hardly likely that such an event would come to pass.

Jesus wanted Nicodemus to see that there are two births: our mother is the agent of our physical birth, and the Holy Spirit is the agent of our spiritual birth. When we were regenerated by the Holy Spirit, we were baptized by the Holy Spirit and became new people (see 1 Cor. 12:13). Unless a person is born supernaturally by the Holy Spirit, he has not experienced salvation, new birth, conversion or regeneration. To be real it must be of the Holy Spirit.

The point was made by D.L. Moody who one day was walking down the street and was accosted by a man deeply under the influence of alcohol. The drunk looked up at Moody through his bloodshot eyes, "You saved me," to which Moody replied, "Yes, you look like one of mine. You weren't saved by Christ!"

The Holy Spirit dwells in believers. At the point of conversion the Holy Spirit takes up His residence in the body of all believers. Second Corinthians 6:16 says, "We are the temple of the living God."

Once again to return to the gifted and greatly used evangelist, D.L. Moody. He tells of burying an aged saint. The elderly deceased man was very poor, but godly and "in line for a great reward." The pallbearers were hastening him off to the grave, wanting to get the service over when an old pastor who was officiating at the grave said, "Tread softly, because you are carrying a temple of the Holy Spirit." Although the church, in its official statements, acknowledges that our bodies are temples of the Holy Spirit, this truth is not frequently allowed to be part of our day-by-day understanding. If we really believed that the living God lives in us we could no longer mistreat our bodies through a lack of sleep, inadequate exercise, improper diet or bad habits.

God in me is a statement full of both hope and challenge: hope because I am His, and challenge to live accordingly.

The Holy Spirit comforts believers. Jesus, in one of His last messages to His disciples, said that the Holy Spirit would come as a helper; that is, He would come to stand alongside as a comforter. In the moments of discouragement and despair, this ministry takes on great meaning. I may go through dark valleys, but He is there with me.

Many summers ago I was driving a taxi in the city of Minneapolis. It was about 11:00 at night when I got a call on my radio to pick up customers at a well-known restaurant. When I arrived at the location, two ladies got in the back seat of the taxi. It was a mother and her daughter who had spent the evening out celebrating a special event. Not only had they eaten well, but they had been drinking. Both were at least moderately drunk.

At such times, customers were often vocal and glib. The mother was no exception to that rule. She asked me, "Cabbie, do you ever get lonely?" I replied immediately that on occasion I do get lonely but I am not alone. She took a quick glance around the cab to see if I had a pet or a passenger that she had not noticed before and replied, "What do you mean?" I told her that the Lord was with me.

I'll never forget her response. "Are you a Baptist?" she asked.

"Yes, I am a Baptist, but more important I am a Christian and Christ through His Holy Spirit is with me at all times," was my reply

The Holy Spirit empowers our witness. If it were not for the fact that the Holy Spirit is in the believer enabling him to bear witness to Christ, there would be no meaningful evangelism (see Acts 1:8). I have seen the Holy Spirit take very shy, unimposing individuals and transform them into radiant, courageous witnesses to the power of Christ. He can do in our lives what we could never do without Him.

Count on it.

God never called you and He never called me to bear witness to ourselves. We are to bear witness to Christ. Nor did God ever tell us that we were to bear witness in our own strength. We have the confident assurance that the Holy Spirit has come to enable the weakest among us to have a wealth of witness that we can share. He will give us the words to say, if we but ask Him.

The Holy Spirit fills believers. In Ephesians 5:18 we are commanded to "be filled with the Spirit." This command is rather confusing to many people. For one reason or another they look on the Holy Spirit in the same way as they look on gasoline in their automobiles. You take a 500-mile trip in your car and it is necessary to fill your tank a couple of times in order to reach your destination. In the same fashion, Christians assume they exhaust the supply of the Holy Spirit in their lives and must have continual refillings. Because the

Holy Spirit is a person and not an influence, the analogy breaks down.

Lewis Sperry Chafer suggests that "To be filled is not the problem of getting *more* of the Spirit; it is rather the problem of the Spirit getting *more* of us. We shall never have more of the Spirit than the anointing which every true Christian has received."[1]

Self-emptying is necessary for the Spirit's filling. We have all of the Holy Spirit. It is not a question of can we have more of Him, but does He have all of us? If we give the Holy Spirit a portion of our life, He can only fill a portion. If we have given Him a half, He will fill us to that degree. If we give Him all of ourselves, He will fill all of us! He fills only that which is emptied for Him.

The Holy Spirit produces godly character. Reflect for a few moments upon the manifestation of the Holy Spirit in the life of a person where God is in control. That life is characterized by "love, joy, peace, patience, kindness, goodness, faithfulness, gentleness, self-control" (Gal. 5:22,23). You will notice that every single one of these items is down-to-earth. There is nothing bizarre or strange about any of them. A person characterized by these virtues would make a great husband or wife, a thoughtful employer, or a magnificent date for a single Christian. Just as you don't append apples to a fig tree, you don't append these virtues to your life. The natural result of the Holy Spirit's control in the life of the believer is a cluster of virtues which comprise the Christian character.

I remember a day in Wisconsin when we had a windstorm. Branches were strewn all about the yards. On the street a number of trees were uprooted and even a couple of roofs were ripped off houses, and I saw three or four chimneys dislodged and lying broken on the ground. I never did see the wind, but I saw its results. The Holy Spirit is invisible to the eye, but His life and His power are to be seen through our character.

It is well for us to remember that the purpose of the Holy Spirit is to glorify Christ in Himself (see John 14:26; 15:26; 16:14). It is unfortunate when the Holy Spirit is on center stage in the Christian's life and experience. That is a new form of unitarianism. When the Holy Spirit fills us and empowers us, the glory belongs to Jesus Christ.

Do you sometimes feel anemic as a Christian? Let me encourage you to yield your life afresh to the Holy Spirit who indwells you. With Him at the helm, we live in victory. Without Him, we are powerless.

You may recall the little skit on "Candid Camera" when a young lady pulled into a service station and asked the attendant to check the oil and water. He lifted the hood and in surprise blurted out, "Madam, you ain't got no motor!" She had everything else. The frame, the seats, the chrome, everything but the power. God the Holy Spirit was given to use us and empower us. Will you allow Him to do just that?

Additional Scriptures
for Study About the Holy Spirit
Nehemiah 9:20
Isaiah 32:15; 59:21
Ezekiel 36:26,27; 39:29
Joel 2:28
Zechariah 4:6
Matthew 3:11; 12:28
Luke 11:13; 12:12
John 7:39; 14:16,17; 16:13
Acts 2:38; 8:39; 10:19,20; 13:2; 16:6
Romans 8:9,11,14,26,27

1 Corinthians 2:12,13; 3:16; 6:19
2 Corinthians 3:5,6
Galatians 5:16-18
2 Timothy 1:14
2 Peter 1:20,21
Revelation 22:17

Footnote

1. Lewis Sperry Chafer, *He That Is Spiritual* (Chicago: Moody Press, 1918), p. 44.

9. We Are God's Special People— in Spite of Our Faults!

"I believe in...the Holy Catholic Church."

God made man for Himself. The chief aim of God in the creation of man was to have a people of whom He could say, "I am theirs and they are mine. I will be their God and they shall be my people." The remarkable story of the Bible is the way in which God still continues with this purpose after, and in spite of, man's falling into sin. God in our day is still forming a people for Himself.

Time after time we read in the Scriptures, "I will take you for My people, and I will be your God" (see Exod. 6:7; Lev. 26:12; Ezek. 11:20). The inspired seer wrote in Revelation 21:2,3: "And I saw the holy city, new Jerusalem, coming

111

down out of heaven from God, made ready as a bride adorned for her husband. And I heard a loud voice from the throne, saying, 'Behold, the tabernacle of God is among men, and He shall dwell among them, and they shall be His peoples, and God Himself shall be among them.' "

When we say that we believe in the Church, we are referring particularly to that body of men and women throughout the ages who have said they are God's people and God is their God. This Church is universal. The word "catholic" really means "universal."

(Perhaps the word "catholic" reminds you of parochial schools, an infallible church and confessionals. But if it does, let me note two things. The Roman Catholic Church today is experiencing some very beautiful life-changing miracles. A concern about personal salvation, a new interest in Bible study and a concern for biblical preaching characterize the Roman Catholic Church in many places. I praise God for this refreshing movement of the Holy Spirit.)

Just because a word is associated with a particular church, we should not limit its meaning. "Catholic" is a good word to describe the Church; for the body of Christ is worldwide, reaching from east to west and encompassing every country of the world. There are no geographical, cultural or ethnic boundaries to the Church of Jesus Christ (see Rev. 5:9). There are Russian Christians, Chinese Christians, African and Brazilian Christians as well as American Christians. Our color, culture and geography may differ, but the common denominator is faith in the person of Jesus Christ, who is Saviour and Lord.

The Meaning of the "Church"

We ought to recognize as we look at the church that this word has a variety of meanings.

Architecturally, the church is a building used for religious functions. In the last three years I have been actively involved with the building committee of the church I serve. We looked for property, purchased a site, received a conditional use permit, worked with an architect to develop a master plan, raised finances and began a building program.

Today the "church" is a split-face building with a tile roof. It accommodates 1100 worshipers in the sanctuary area on the second level and has additional Christian education space on the lower level. When I think of the "church," I cannot help but think of a building located at 8175 Villaverde, Whittier, California, 90605. All across our world the word "church" has this same connotation. It is a building used for the purposes of worship and instruction.

Church has a sociological meaning. David O. Moberg says that the "church" is "a major social institution in America."[1] As a social institution the church can be studied in terms of its age-sex profile, its leadership, its financial situation and all of its observable functions and dysfunctions. When the church is viewed sociologically, it can be compared to groups, fraternities, sororities and other groupings of people.

When we look at the "church" as a building or as an institution, we use a small "c."

Biblically, Church becomes big "C." The Church is a spiritual reality. It is a worldwide body of believers in Jesus Christ. Paul Minear tells us that there are at least 100 different words for "church" in the New Testament.[2] Among the most familiar synonyms for "church" are the following:

1. Fellowship—All kinds of Sunday School classes and Christian groups in recent years have taken on the title of *Koinonia.* Perhaps you are aware of the fact that this is the Greek New Testament word for fellowship (see 1 John 1:7).

113

The church I pastor is called the Whittier Area Baptist Fellowship. Each of the words in our title has a particular significance. We are called Whittier to designate the particular city in which we are located. The word "Area" is used to suggest that we are a regional church and not limited in ministry to only a city. Baptist is in our title because of our historical persuasion regarding Baptist distinctives. And we are called a fellowship because it indicates a warm, intimate relation enjoyed by the people of God with their Lord and with one another.

Three years ago a number of us appeared before the City Council of Whittier to defend our right to a conditional use permit in order to build. A number of folks voiced opposition to our project. They said it would create traffic problems, it would affect property values of homes in the community in the area of the church and it would hurt the tax benefits that come into the city from that 17-acre plot of land.

We responded to each of them in order, with a traffic consultant, an appraiser and a tax consultant. The evidences were in our favor. However, in the hearing I was startled to hear one of the opponents of our project say, "They aren't even a church. They are a fellowship." After the others had testified in our favor, I spoke to the question of whether or not we were a church and explained, "We have chosen a 1900-year-old synonym for church. The Bible uses that word to identify the church and we have chosen it because it expresses the identity of people who share a relationship with one another as members of the body of Christ."

If the Church is anything, it is at least a fellowship and it ought to be a fellowship characterized by a "sweet, sweet spirit," as one of our contemporary songs describes it.

2. Saints—First Corinthians 1:2 refers to the Church of

God as those who are saints by calling. To be a saint is to be a holy one, which is what we are "in Christ." It is easy enough to point out that we are not always saintly. We sometimes yell at each other at our church business meetings, lose our temper at church committee meetings, use the phone to gossip about a deacon and sit around the Sunday dinner table and have roast preacher.

How well we know that the saints are not always saintly! We are saints only because of God's action "in Christ," not because of our action in the flesh.

3. Believers—The Church is a company of people who have faith in Christ. John 1:12 says, "But as many as received Him, to them He gave the right to become children of God, even to those who believe in His name."

I recall a conversation in my office one day when I asked a counselee, "Are you going to heaven when you die?" She replied, "Yes." When I inquired further as to what basis, she replied, "I live by the Ten Commandments and the Golden Rule." Her response was no different than that which every witness for Christ has heard on one occasion or another. The only appropriate response, of course, is that I will go to heaven when I die because I have trusted Jesus Christ as my personal Saviour. The Church is made up of believers.

4. Servants—The same word which is translated "servant" in the New Testament can also be translated "slave." Strange as it seems, our true freedom is found in bondage or servitude to Jesus. It was Paul in his letter to the Corinthians who said, "For we do not preach ourselves but Christ Jesus as Lord, and ourselves as your bond-servants for Jesus' sake (2 Cor. 4:5). The concept of bond-servants expresses both a relationship of dependence and a duty of obedience. It is a privilege of the believer to serve and obey his Lord.

5. The people of God—The people of God are united

across the periods of the Old and the New Testament. First Peter 2:9 speaks of us as "a chosen race, a royal priesthood, a holy nation, a people for God's own possession."

In Paul's letter to the church at Rome, he reminded them that the people of God can be likened to an olive tree. It includes both Jews who were a part of the natural tree and Gentiles who were grafted in to make a "cultivated" olive tree. Paul was trying to impress upon his readers that Christians in the first century had a continuity with Abraham, David, and Elijah and all of the Old Testament saints who trusted God (see Heb. 11:6; Rom 1:16,17).

6. Family—The Church is variously described as sons (Heb. 2:10), brothers (1 Pet. 2:17), and as the bride (John 3:29). All three of these pictures speak of the intimacy we have with each other and with our heavenly Father.

The experience I have with my dad, which I think is healthy, has been marked by love and openness. He has shared his dreams with me, has challenged me and shown loving concern for me. I in turn have sought to seek his advice, follow his counsel and be an obedient heir. Anybody who knows us would remind you that our relationship has not been perfect, but by the same token not bad!

The parallelism is rather clear. God is the Father and we are His children. The best of father-son relationships that you and I can experience are but a mere shadow of that which exists between God and the children of God. The metaphor just starts us off in the right direction. It is a point of reference from the human side which helps us to understand what we have in our relationship to God.

7. The Body of Christ—Perhaps the best term for the Church, the one used most often, is that of the body of Christ. First Corinthians 12:12 teaches that the "body is one and yet has many members, and all the members of the

body, though they are many, are one body." Christ is the head of the body and we are the members.

A friend once quipped as I left his home, "Bless your heart and all your other moving parts." Not a bad line. Our body is a miraculous creation of God. It has a splendid variety with its eyes, its ears, its hands, its feet, its nose, mouth and multiple organs. The one thing I have noticed about my body is that what affects one part of the body affects the whole body.

For eight years our family lived in Minnesota. I remember a period of about 10 days in January which got so cold that it almost never went above zero degrees, not even in the warmest part of the afternoon. You could bundle up in a snowmobile outfit, goggles, fur cap, snowmobile boots and gloves—but just to have your nose exposed to the cold somehow sent a chill through the whole body. The same thing occurred during our rainy season. I could have an umbrella and raincoat, but if my feet got wet, the whole body seemed to feel the chill.

The point applies to the Church. We are one body in Christ. When one part of the body is infirmed, the entire Church feels the sickness. When one member of the body is in sin, the rest of the body is negatively affected.

But by the same token, when one member is enjoying health and vitality, the rest of the body rejoices together with it!

The Characteristics of the Church

It is possible to be baptized by the church, be an active worshiper in the church, serve as an officer and tithe your income to the church and still not be a part of *the* Church. As good as each of those items may be, it in no way qualifies a person for inclusion in the body of Christ.

The Church is a redeemed community. Jesus is spoken of as the "Saviour of the body." The word "Church" occurs over 100 times in the New Testament. The *ecclesia* means "called out"—that is to say, the Church is made up of individuals who have been called by God and have responded in faith.

A gifted young attorney I know in his mid-thirties had a lovely family, a lovely wife, healthy children, a thriving vocation and a nice home in a beautiful community. One day he learned that a fellow attorney friend had committed suicide. He reasoned to himself that if that man did not have it "all together" neither did he. It was only a matter of weeks after attending an evangelical church and studying the Scriptures that he accepted the crucified and risen Christ as Saviour and Lord of his life. The pattern is common to all members of the Church. They recognize that they are inadequate in themselves and that Jesus Christ is supremely adequate.

When you read the book of Acts, you discover that Christians are ordinary men and women who, with all their faults and follies, made contact with the living Christ and became a new people. The Church is a redeemed community, made up of sinners saved by grace, not good people who deserve it (see Eph. 2:8,9).

The Church is a caring community. A careful reading of 1 John reveals that it is impossible to love God and not love our brother. In Christ we are one; when one member suffers, the body is to respond. The concerns of one become the concerns of the group.

When Dr. Bruce Thielemann was pastor of the Glendale Presbyterian Church, he was invited to preach at the Presidential Prayer Breakfast in Washington, D.C. Prior to his trip to the East Coast he told his congregation of his fears and asked for their prayerful support. He went to Washington and prepared for the momentous occasion. He arose early and reviewed his sermon a number of times. The phone rang and it was a gentleman at the front desk who informed Dr. Thielemann that he had a telegram.

Dr. Thielemann inquired who the sender was. The man at the desk replied, "I am afraid I can't tell you that, but I can give you the message."

Thielemann thought to himself, "That is strange. Why can't he tell me who it is from?" But he asked for the message.

The deskman said the message said simply, "We love you," and included more than 300 signatures. The gifted Presbyterian preacher went to the Prayer Breakfast greatly encouraged because he knew of their love and their prayers. They were ministering to his need.

The Christian can never be an island. He can and must be a peninsula, with a bridge that connects him with the mainland of the Christian Church. If we are to be known as a caring people, it is necessary that we share our lives with each other. I would encourage you to read again that helpful volume by Keith Miller, *Taste of New Wine*.[3] This book became an instant best-seller among Christians because Miller said things that many of us had thought about but did not have the courage to say. He took off his mask and allowed himself to risk vulnerability—the price we all must pay if we are to really share and care for each other. When we run around roleplaying and living superficially, we find little encouragement from each other.

If we are to care, we first must share.

The Church is a worshiping community. The Church is made up of groups of people who join together to recognize the worth-ship of God. Christians ought to become worshipers before they become workers.

The sixth chapter of Isaiah has served as a model for many congregations. Worship includes *adoration*—"Holy, Holy, Holy, is the Lord of hosts" (Isa. 6:3); *confession*—"Woe is me, for I am ruined! Because I am a man of unclean lips, and I live among a people of unclean lips; For my eyes have seen the King, the Lord of hosts" (Isa. 6:5); *the assurance of forgiveness*—"And he touched my mouth with it [burning coal] and said, 'Behold, this has touched your lips; and your iniquity is taken away, and your sin is forgiven' " (Isa. 6:7); *instruction*—The voice of the Lord spoke to Isaiah the prophet (see Isa. 6:9-13); *response*—When the Lord asked the question, "Whom shall I send, and who will go for Us?" Isaiah responded, "Here am I. Send me!" (Isa. 6:8).

Healthy Christians recognize the need for attending a place of worship on a regular basis. While it may be true that some Christians can worship God in the mountains, on the beach or on the golf course, it is less likely to occur than in the midst of a people who are singing, praying, and listening to the Scriptures being expounded!

I would encourage you to read *All Originality Makes a Dull Church*[4] to see the variety of forms that a worship-community can take in the local situation.

The Church is a witnessing community. The Church gathers together for the purpose of worship, instruction and encouragement, and is dispersed into the world in order to witness. Jesus said that Christians are the light of the world (Matt. 5:14) and in this capacity they crowd out the darkness and bring light to a sinful world. Christians are also the salt of the earth (Matt. 5:13) and as such exist in the world to give it zest and tastefulness. Nothing is quite so bland as good food that is unsalted. The world needs the Church. Some Christians will have the gift of evangelism, but every Christian is called to bear witness—by word and by life.

The late Sir Thomas Lipton, Britain's millionaire grocer, began his business with a small shop in Glasgow. Soon he had scores of stores all over Britain. His success was the result of press-agentry. "Laddie," he once told a young boy, "it is like this: When a chicken lays an egg, she cackles an' tells the whole farmyard. But when a duck lays an egg, she makes no' a sound. An' how many people eat ducks' eggs?" Sir Lipton's formula for success, it will be no surprise to learn was, "He who on his trade relies must either bust or advertise."

In this modern age of advertising it is sometimes difficult to understand why the Church has played the part of the duck and done so little witnessing to the truth. We are a group of people committed to the task of communicating the gospel to a skeptical, materialistic age. There is small place for a silent Christianity.

At other times our witness will be by life. A strong Christian influence has been left by Christians who have no other distinguishing mark than the simple contagion of Christ's influence through their lives. While our lives may not always reflect the Christ we serve, it ought to be the goal for each of us that when someone discovers that we are Christians, they do not reply, "Wow! I never would have guessed that!" Instead, we want them to say, "Well, that makes sense. I knew there was something about you that was different."

You are the Church. Wherever you are, there is the Church. The Church is not limited to a building, an institution, or a location. A number of us meet for prayer each week to remember the members of our congregation. When we pray we remember the Church that is meeting in the office, in the classroom, in the kitchen and on the freeway. Our prayer for them and I hope your prayer for us is that the church (c) will be the Church (C).

God has always had a people. Many a foolish conqueror has made the mistake of thinking that because he has driven the Church of Jesus Christ out of sight that he has stilled its voice and snuffed out its life.

But God has always had a people. The powerful current of a rushing river is not diminished because it is forced to flow underground. The purest water is the stream that bursts crystal clear into the sunlight after it has fought its way through solid rock. There have been charlatans who, like Simon the magician, sought to barter on the open market that power which cannot be bought or sold. But God has always had a people: Men who could not be bought and women who are beyond purchase. God has always had a people. There have been times of affluence and prosperity when the church's message has been nearly diluted into oblivion by those who sought to make it socially attractive, neatly organized, and financially profitable. It has been gold-plated, draped in purple, and encrusted with jewels.

It has been misrepresented, ridiculed, lauded, and scorned. These followers of Jesus Christ have been according to the whim of the time, elevated as sacred leaders and martyred as heretics. Yet, through it all, there marches on that powerful army of the meek—

God's chosen people, who could not be bought, murdered, martyred, or stilled. On through the ages they march—the Church—God's Church—triumphant —alive, and well.[5]

Additional Scriptures
for Study About the Church
Matthew 16:16-18
Romans 12:4,5
1 Corinthians 3:10; 12:27
Ephesians 1:22,23; 2:19-22; 4:11,12
Colossians 1:24

Footnotes

1. David O. Moberg, *The Church As a Social Institution* (Englewood Cliffs, New Jersey: Prentice-Hall, Inc., 1962), p. 1.
2. Buttrick, *The Interpreter's Dictionary of the Bible*, Vol. 1, p. 617.
3. Keith Miller, *Taste of New Wine* (Waco, Texas: Word Books, 1966).
4. Dan Baumann, *All Originality Makes a Dull Church* (Santa Ana, California: Vision House Publishers, 1976).
5. William J. and Gloria Gaither, "The Church Triumphant," © Copyright 1973 by William J. Gaither, from songbook *Something Beautiful No. 2*, 1975 (Alexandria, Indiana: Gaither Music Co.), pp. 42,43.

10. We Can't Get Along with Them; We Can't Get Along Without Them!

"I believe in...the communion of the saints."

William Glasser, the well-known psychologist, has written that we have passed through what he calls the "civilized survival society" which he believes lasted from about 10,000 years ago until 1950. For that extended period, man's primary struggle was to survive. He was concerned with questions like, "What is going to be my occupation? How am I going to care for my family? How am I going to be a success?" Glasser theorizes that about 1950, the primary question for most people became, "Who am I? I want to know my identity. I want to be a part of my society, a group, a community, where people are discovering who they are."[1]

In the midst of this newly-felt need sits the community of God's people. Although the need is current, the communion of saints extends back some 1900 years. Jesus Christ, through His death and resurrection, brought into being a company of people who are discovering the meaning of life and who celebrate that meaning together.

Christian community formed solely on Jesus Christ is discussed in John 17. Jesus, in His High Priestly prayer said, "I do not ask in behalf of these alone, but for those also who believe in Me through their word; that they may all be one; even as Thou, Father, art in Me, and I in Thee, that they also may be in Us; that the world may believe that Thou didst send Me. And the glory which Thou hast given Me I have given to them; that they may be one, just as We are one; I in them, and Thou in Me, that they may be perfected in unity, that the world may know that Thou didst send Me, and didst love them, even as Thou didst love Me" (John 17:20-23).

We discover in 1 John 1 that fellowship is first of all with our heavenly Father and secondly with fellow Christians. John wrote, "Our fellowship is with the Father, and with His Son, Jesus Christ" (1 John 1:3). Pointedly, John adds, "But if we walk in the light as He Himself is in the light, we have fellowship with one another" (v. 7). The concern of Jesus in John 17 and the God-ordained reality in 1 John has wide ramifications; the wider fellowship of Christians everywhere, and the closer fellowship of Christians within certain geographical boundaries.

Wider Fellowship

I believe that we ought to have fellowship with all Christians regardless of denominational differences. Provincialism and petty spirit are a scandal to the known Christian world. Some of the petty differences between Christians invite criticism from unbelievers. When the world looks in through our stained glass windows and observes that Christians are separated from one another or warring against each other, much of our potential ministry is spoiled. A

126

displeasure with some of the policies of national and international organizations in an attempt to achieve organizational unity does not mean that we oppose true oneness. We have an ecumenical oneness, according to the Scriptures.

First of all, we have a common Lord (see Eph. 4:5). Although Episcopalians and Pentecostals might be uncomfortable in each other's churches due to the form and expression of faith, if they both know Jesus Christ as Saviour and Lord they are to be united in Christ. I find it difficult to believe that people can stand at the foot of the cross and not link hands and hearts with other believers. Most of the things which divide Christians are incidental in contrast to the major truth which unites us, namely, the person of Jesus Christ.

Biblical oneness is further based upon a common faith (see Eph. 4:5). Christians are individuals whose sins have been cleansed through the shed blood of Jesus Christ. When I partake of communion with fellow Baptists in Whittier, I am at one with others who take communion—Presbyterians in New York, Nazarenes in Kansas City, and Mennonite Brethren in Windom, Minnesota. We are part of a world-wide, blood-cleansed fellowship! Our faith is not in our policy, our forms of worship or denominational distinctives; rather, it is in Jesus Christ and the salvation purchased through His death and resurrection.

A common task ties us together biblically, too. The purpose of every Christian group is to build the body of Christ until it attains its maturity (see Eph. 4:12,13). The task of witnessing to the world in the power of the Holy Spirit is not reserved for one little corner of the Kingdom of God. It belongs to all who call Christ Lord, and this witness is to be shared in every corner of the world (see Acts 1:8).

Biblical oneness doesn't require a world church, though some fear this possibility. Such a plan would create a monolithic organization full of power and structure and not necessarily committed to the Great Commission.

It seems, though, that *some* variety is appropriate. There are individuals who personally need a liturgical form of worship, while others' needs are best met through an informal expression of Christian worship.

I recall a banquet I attended in Chicago a number of years ago at which a well-known Southern evangelist graphically portrayed what would happen if an Episcopal attended a typical Pentecostal service. He said, "Our Episcopal brother would dissolve in flames. On the other hand if the Pentecostal Christian would attend an Episcopal service," said the evangelist, "they would carry him out stiff as a board."

The point is well taken: although both the true Episcopals and Pentecostals know and love Jesus Christ, they have distinct ways in which they like to express that love when they are gathered together with fellow Christians. In one congregation there will be litany, liturgy, choral response, recitation of the Apostles' Creed and great significance placed upon the sacraments. In the other setting, the service may be regularly syncopated with "Hallelujah," "Praise God," and "Amen," from the congregation; the pastor's prayer may be accompanied by others praying aloud within the congregation. It would seem foolish to suggest that one is right and one is wrong—they are simply ways in which differing personality needs are met. Our only concern would be regarding the biblical integrity of the message, not the form in which our Lord is worshiped.

Biblical oneness does not require a "lowest common denominator theology." Unity at the expense of biblical purity is too great a price to pay. Basic scriptural truths *cannot* be surrendered. The cardinal doctrines of the Christian faith—an inspired Bible, sinfulness of man, the virgin birth of Christ, His vicarious atonement, the bodily resurrection of Christ, salvation by faith alone and an eternal heaven and hell—must be maintained for the sake of the gospel. When these truths are held in common with other Christians, regardless of their denomination, we are one in spirit, purpose and ministry.

There are three implications to the wider fellowship I have just discussed:

1. Pray for and with other Christians. Some of our fellow believers are in very difficult situations. In 1967, 23 of us visited Christian "high points" in Europe. We arrived in Leipzig, East Germany on a Saturday night. I went down to the police station with our English-speaking tour guide and we registered the names and passports of our group. The following morning we shared in a worship service in a small banquet room provided by the hotel. It was in a setting I will never forget. A police guard was stationed at the door and monitored our service. A microphone in the ceiling recorded our music, testimonies and sermon. Years later a member of the group, a printer by vocation, mentioned that one of the highlights of his life was praying at that service in a city famous in our Protestant tradition, but now under Communist control.

During this same tour we met a Lutheran pastor in Eisleben, the birthplace of Martin Luther. This pastor believed in Scriptures to be true and preached a simple, gospel message in the midst of state-wide atheism and Communist control. Americans know little of the oppression and pressure faced by fellow Christians, whether in East Germany, China, Russia or Vietnam.

2. Visit with other Christians. Every other week I share

129

lunch with two fellow pastors: one a Presbyterian and one a Congregationalist. The fellowship we experience around the table has enlarged my vision and enriched my life. They are both committed to evangelism, the biblical message and obedience to Christ. They allow me to stretch beyond the parochial confines of my own denomination. While I believe in what my denomination stands for and support it enthusiastically, I need the stretching and enlargement of vision that other Christians in other traditions can provide.

Interdenominational Christian colleges have provided a beautiful laboratory in which young, thoughtful evangelicals have benefited from this exposure. The experience allows the participant to grow and to see that God cannot be limited within our favored categories.

3. Join with other Christians in worthy projects. Many things have been accomplished in the last couple of decades that would have been impossible without Christians of varied traditions joining together to make them a reality. For example, the Billy Graham Crusades are dependent upon prayer support, financial undergirding and commitment of Christians with greatly varied backgrounds and affiliations. To me, there is nothing quite like the experience of joining 125,000 people in Chicago's Soldiers Field to listen to a crusade choir sing, to listen to the testimonies of well-known public figures and to hear the Holy Spirit-empowered preaching of Billy Graham. Perhaps most thrilling of all is to see hundreds make their way to the front of the stadium to profess faith in Jesus Christ.

I have attended perhaps a dozen Billy Graham Crusade meetings and have never stood through an invitation without getting goosebumps. I thank God that He raised up Billy Graham as a spokesman for the good news in our day. He has reached millions of people through his worldwide telecasts and printed ministry. Can you imagine how little of this would have been accomplished if Billy Graham had limited the scope of his ministry to a single denomination?

Youth for Christ, Young Life, Campus Crusade and Intervarsity Fellowship have ministries with high school and college students all across our nation. They deserve our prayerful and financial support. The combined efforts of Christians greatly increase evangelistic effectiveness on the campuses across America. In many cases they reach young people who would otherwise never hear.

You could add illustrations of your own to document the point I am making: the communion of saints means we are one in spirit and purpose with others who are committed to Jesus Christ as Saviour and Lord.

The Closer Fellowship

The communion of saints applies to those who are part of the local fellowship—as a Christian I am related to all the members of my local church. This carries with it certain pleasures and responsibilities.

We are to help others. Dietrich Bonhoeffer says we must allow ourselves to be "interrupted" by God. "God will be constantly crossing our paths and cancelling our plans by sending us people with claims and petitions."[2]

Jesus set the pattern by His own example of thoughtfulness and helpfulness. I do not recall a single situation of need that came to the attention of Jesus where He did not step in to minister help, healing or encouragement. When those about Him were sick, He healed them. When they were blind, He made them to see. When they were hungry, He performed a miracle and fed them—4,000 on one occasion and 5,000 on another.

Acts 4:34,35 tells us that the early church pooled its

131

resources in order to meet the needs of the others. Some sold land and houses and brought the profits of the sales to the apostles. The money was then distributed to the needy. This demonstration of selflessness and love sometimes is difficult for us to initiate. We sometimes build fences around our property, describing an attitude and spirit of "you live your life and I will live mine. Please do not trespass. If you have needs, that is up to you to cover. If I have needs, I will make it on my own." Sometimes in our own sufficiency we find it difficult to accept help and in our selfishness, to extend help.

In March, 1973, Lindon Karo, my former student, later my own pastor and personal friend, died of cancer and left behind a wife and three children. During his illness he preached a series of sermons at the Salem Baptist Church in New Brighton, Minnesota on the Apostles' Creed. His last sermon prior to his death was on the communion of saints. In it he described a personal experience:

> I had a bad experience one day this week in the hospital.
> My right eye was hemorrhaging, and they wanted me to go down to the eye clinic and have it checked out.
> I waited two and one-half hours in the hallway in a wheelchair.
> Nobody seemed to care about me or others waiting there.
> Finally, I was examined and began to leave.
> In the process I got into a different-colored wheelchair than the one that was assigned to the seventh floor.
> Suddenly a nurse came running after us, saying, "I have to have this wheelchair back. It belongs here."
> At that moment I felt that they were more concerned about their wheelchair than the patient in it.
> But we easily fall into the same sin.

132

We tend to care more about possessions than we care about people.

The early Christians didn't only *say* they were God's people; they showed it by selling what they had and distributing it as people had need.[3]

We are to bear one another's burdens. Paul wrote to the church at Galatia and encouraged them to bear one another's burdens and thus fulfill the law of Christ (Gal. 6:2). When we became Christians, we not only accepted Jesus Christ as our Saviour, but we accepted the body of Christ. We belong to Christ and to each other. When any part of the body is needy, broken, hurt, anxious or grieving, it is our responsibility to lovingly help shoulder the load. My wife, Nancy, does this exceptionally well. On many an occasion she has gone to an individual who has just gone through a crisis such as a loss of a loved one or the discovery of cancer and has talked and listened and cried with them. Very often the ministry of bearing is accomplished by simply putting our arms around a fellow Christian, blending our tears together and finding the strength that comes from Christian presence.

A plaque in our family room underscores my point: "A sorrow that's shared is but half a trouble; but a joy that's shared is a joy made double."

Recently my congregation has been struck with multiple instances of cancer. I am without easy answers and perplexed as to why godly people should have to suffer as they do. And yet, I acknowledge that God is sovereign; disease is not a judgment from God, and His grace *is* sufficient. I have been greatly encouraged to discover that Christians rally around their brothers and sisters, write notes of encouragement, call to express concern, visit, and provide meals as well as offer rides for those in need. The shared strength that the stricken have experienced is a beautiful testimony of the reality of the communion of saints. I do not know what a person without Christ does in times of extreme illness, grief or depression.

You may recall that the apostle Paul had an infirmity that God chose not to heal: "There was given me a thorn in the flesh, a messenger of Satan to buffet me—to keep me from exalting myself! Concerning this I entreated the Lord three times that it might depart from me" (2 Cor. 12:7,8). Our Lord graciously provided two things: grace that was sufficient and a companion like Luke.

We are to lend an ear. You and I both know many individuals who have or are paying for a psychiatrist, psychologist or counselor. These individuals need someone with whom they can share. On many occasions the greatest need of the counselee is not so much personal and professional advice and direction as it is love, understanding and a listening ear. We need to remind ourselves that our brethren in Christ often need our ear just as we on occasion need theirs.

It is not easy to listen. Not only are we impatient, self-centered and inattentive by nature, but often we have never been trained to listen. During our school years we are taught to write. In the Chicago public schools where I attended during my grammar school days, I practiced the Palmer Method of handwriting by the hour. My teachers were convinced that my future usefulness in the world was dependent upon my ability to write. After I had learned the mechanical part of writing, I was assigned hundreds and hundreds of written projects, from quizzes to term papers to finally a doctoral dissertation. My education was geared to helping me write and express myself in print.

By the time I was in third grade I had learned to read. It

was slow going at first as I inched my way into primers. Miss Pedigrew, my first grade teacher, practically despaired during those early months of my reading education. Today I read magazines, journals and books with ease. The reason is that I was taught how to read and even how to comprehend what I was reading.

Typically, I had two or three required speech courses before I was permitted to graduate from high school. With knocking knees, sweaty palms and shaking voice I delivered my stumbling oratory. At the end of each speech I vowed that I would never again speak in public. But God took what I identified as weakness and called me to preach!

Almost everyone else in America has had a similar experience to mine: we were taught to write, to read and somewhat to speak—but how many of us have ever had a course in listening? And yet researchers tell us that most of communication is listening, not writing, reading or speaking.

Let me encourage you to do what I have tried to do—to concentrate when people speak, and listen attentively until they are finished. It is very easy to listen with half an ear to assume that we have heard it all before and assume that the speaker doesn't need our undivided attention. All too often we wait for the speaker to take a breath—*and we jump!* In the process we deny a friend our thoughtfulness. The ministry of listening has been entrusted to us by the Lord, who Himself is the perfect listener (see Ps. 91:15). We need to continually lend an ear.

We are to instruct each other. Mature Christians have the responsibility of teaching the newer, less mature believers. Paul, who had instructed Timothy as his own disciple, told him it was his privilege to spare what he had learned with "faithful men, who will be able to teach others also" (2 Tim. 2:2).

Some have gone so far as to suggest that every Christian ought to be either a discipler or a disciple—teaching someone or being instructed by someone. The implication is that truths learned are not only to be retained but communicated and shared with others.

Instruction takes place for the Christian in two important locations: in the church with fellow members of the body of Christ who are part of our spiritual family, and in the home with our own family. The goal for Christians should be to move from spiritual infancy through adolescence into adulthood. Paul expressed this goal very clearly: "We proclaim Him, admonishing every man and teaching every man with all wisdom, that we may present every man complete in Christ" (Col. 1:28).

The communion of saints is not reserved for those who are our friends; the communion of saints is to exist between all members of the body of Christ. In order to help you achieve this goal you might benefit from the exercise used by Billy Kim, Pastor of the Central Baptist Church, Suwan, Korea, and the members of his congregation who are working on a "Christian Love Explosion." It has seven requirements:

1. Read 1 Corinthians 13 once every day.

2. Pray for someone you resent.

3. For one week refuse to think any negative thoughts about anyone.

4. For one week do not say anything negative about anyone to anyone.

5. Think of as many positive, good explanations for the behavior of others as you can.

6. Listen with interest and compassion to someone you consider boring at least once a week.

7. Do a good deed (anonymously) for someone you hate.[4]

It is both a privilege and a responsibility to be a part of the Christian community. Not only are we in Christ and are to live for Him, but we are co-members with all other Christians and are to live for each other.

Lindon Karo concluded his last sermon prior to his premature death at the age of 32: "It is great to be a saint and to have communion with one another. It is holy communion, a special type of communion set apart for the people of God."[5]

Additional Scriptures
to Study About the Communion of the Saints
Psalm 119:63
Malachi 3:16
Acts 2:41-47
Romans 1:11,12; 12:4,5
1 Corinthians 1:10
2 Corinthians 13:11
Galatians 3:28
Ephesians 4:1-4
Philippians 1:3-7,27; 4:2,3
Colossians 2:1,2
1 Peter 3:8,9

Footnotes

1. William Glasser, *The Identity Society* (New York: Harper & Row, Publishers, Inc., 1972).
2. Dietrich Bonhoeffer, *Life Together* (New York: Harper & Row, Publishers, 1954), p. 99.
3. Nancy Karo (with Alvera Mickelsen), *Adventure in Dying* (Chicago: Moody Press, Moody Bible Institute of Chicago 1976), p. 194. Used by permission.
4. From the Log of the Good Ship Grace, September, 1976, Vol. 42, No. 18.
5. Karo, *Adventure in Dying*, pp. 198,199.

11. Wow! What a Relief!

"I believe in...the forgiveness of sins."

During the springtime of my fifth grade I was returning home from school. Another buddy and I were playing catch across the street from each other. Both of us had strong arms, but we suffered the same problem—inaccuracy.

We had been playing for a couple of blocks when I threw a ball across the street way over my friend's head and through the glass front door of a neighbor's home. The smashing of that window sent a chill up my spine. I walked slowly across the street, moved gingerly up the doorstep, rang the bell and said to myself, "I hope they aren't home" and sure enough, they weren't.

I returned home, told my mom about my plight. She encouraged me to try a bit later. It was just about the supper

139

hour when I rang the door bell once again. This time the lady of the house was home. "My name is Dan Baumann," I stammered. "I threw the ball through your window. I am very sorry. I would like to pay to have it fixed."

She said, "Wait here a minute." Returning a few moments later with a dustpan and a broom, she asked me to clean up the broken glass. I did, handed her the loaded dustpan and asked what I owed her. Much to my surprise she said, "Young man, I appreciate your honesty. You owe me nothing. Thanks for telling me what you had done." Not only that, but she gave me a candy bar.

I could hardly wait to get home and report in to my folks. Mom heard me coming down the sidewalk and knew immediately that everything had been cared for. I whistled all the way home. I felt so good, so clean. I was forgiven.

Of all the feelings and emotions experienced by human beings, I find none so liberating, cleansing and satisfying as that of being forgiven. Christians believe in a God who forgives. The Bible pictures God as one whose heart of love expresses itself in forgiveness to man.

An East Coast preacher once began his sermon, "My message this morning is only for sinners. If you are not a sinner, my message is not for you. However, if you are a sinner, I have good news. I want to talk about forgiveness." Isaiah wrote, "All of us like sheep have gone astray" (Isa. 53:6). The message of forgiveness is a theme with a *universal* application.

Is Forgiveness Necessary?

Suppose I tell a man that the essential thing about the gospel is that Christ offers forgiveness. Suppose I tell him that God through Christ can forgive him. And he replies, "There is some mistake! Christ has come to the wrong

140

address. Forgiveness? For me? What do I need it for? No doubt there are plenty of others who have blundered and made a mess of things. That is why the world is in such a sorry state . . . But me? What have I done, that I should need forgiveness?"

That same man may continue, "Do you think that God is going to care how I choose to run my life? He has more important things to do. The Power behind the universe just pats the sinner on the back and says, 'There, there. You did not mean it. It does not matter!' Therefore forgiveness is not necessary. Offer it to others who need it, but don't bother me with something I don't need."

How do we reply to this logic?

If there is no sin problem, then the whole question of forgiveness is irrelevant. James Stuart Stewart, the Scottish preacher, says that there are three facts that destroy the illusion that forgiveness is unnecessary.[1]

Sin takes on reality when we look at the chaos of the world. In the *Whittier Daily News* which came to our door this evening, the following items are included on a single page: three men were in police custody today on charges of twice burglarizing a clothing store; two teenagers are in custody with shoplifting charges; officers reported the theft of an automobile; two juveniles took a purse away from a 57-year-old woman. In addition, our small city reported four petty thefts and three burglaries—a rather typical day for a community of 75,000 people.

But that is just the start. Man's inhumanity to man has been expressed thousands of times between an employer and an employee, fellow students, a child and his parents, and one selfish driver to another. The judgment of the Scriptures rings true around us in every city of the world. "There is none righteous, not even one" (Rom. 3:10) and

141

"all have sinned and fall short of the glory of God" (Rom. 3:23).

Sin takes on reality when we contrast God and man. "He had a daily beauty in his life" said Iago of Cassio in *Othello,* "that makes me ugly." In the presence of our Lord, we feel the same, even more. When the prophet saw the Lord in the temple, he experienced the great distance that separated him from a holy God. When he saw the Lord who was holy he exclaimed, "Woe is me, for I am ruined! Because I am a man of unclean lips, And I live among a people of unclean lips; for my eyes have seen the King, the Lord of hosts" (Isa. 6:5).

Sin takes on reality when we look at the cross of Christ. The common sins of our everyday life, are the nails that were plunged into His holy body at Calvary (see Rom. 5:8). The supreme price that Christ paid demands that there be a great problem! Only the reality of sin makes it logical.

It may be helpful for us to define sin, to help clear up our misconceptions. One way to define sin is to call it, "Any act or attitude, personal or social that fails to express love for God, neighbor or self." The two great commandments are to love God and our neighbor as ourselves (see Matt. 22:37-39). Whenever we act in such a way that we are not loving to our creator or our neighbor, we have fallen into sin. The Ten Commandments involve either a failure to love God (commandments 1-4), or a failure to love neighbor (commandments 5-10). We can ask ourselves at any point of our life, is our attitude or action loving or sinful?

Another way to define sin is to look at the biblical word *hamartia,* which means "to miss the mark." Sin is any lack of complete conformity to the will of God; it is falling short of the divine standard which is perfect and absolute.

The story is told of a volcano which was spitting forth lava

142

that produced an avalanche. Two men were fleeing for their lives in the only possible direction of safety. However, as they ran, they came upon a turbulent stream. Their only hope was to jump across it, a total of 50 feet. The one man who was a track star and could broad jump 25 feet laughed at the other man who was handicapped by arthritis and could only jump a few feet. As the avalanche approached they both jumped. One jumped only a few feet, the other 26 feet, but both were beaten to death against the sharp rocks by the turbulent waters. To be sure, one was closer to safety than the other, but both fell short of the required distance, the standard, of 50 feet.

Although I cannot vouch for the historical truth of the above story, it does express in subtle form the truth of Romans 3:23. Every man falls short. God's standard is perfection.

Some sin is very obvious. Just today I heard individuals swearing, cussing out their parents and admitting to adultery. These sins are obvious and unfortunately common. All three of them break the Ten Commandments.

Some sins, however, are not so obvious. There are *sins of the temperament.* Jesus' parable of the Prodigal Son portrays the delight of the parent when his wayward son returned home. There was gaiety, singing and visiting because the prodigal had returned. It was said of his elder brother that "he became angry" (Luke 15:28). Anger along with such things as envy, bitterness and bad temper are sins of the temperament.

Another less obvious sin is the *sin of neglect.* Think of these two well-known parables. The first is the parable of the talents that tells of the man who hid his one talent in the ground. What did he do? That was the trouble. He did nothing. He missed his chance. The second parable is about

143

the good Samaritan. What was the trouble with the priest and the Levite who left the victim on the road between Jericho and Jerusalem? What did they do? That was the difficulty—they did nothing; they went by on the other side.

There are also *sins of faulty motivation.* One can do a good deed but for the wrong reason. The hypocrites, a common subject considered by Jesus, loved to stand and pray in the synagogue and on the street corners in order to be seen by men. Their motivation was pride. To be sure, they were praying; but it was all performance and show.

If you add the sins of temperament, neglect and faulty motivation to the sins of the flesh with the common lists of sins (Ten Commandments and Golden Rule), you begin to see that forgiveness is not a luxury reserved for a few but a necessity for all of us. We all need forgiveness.

Sin follows the path of least resistance like the Jordan River which meanders for 200 miles when a straight line between the Sea of Galilee and the Dead Sea would only measure 55 miles. Sin is the outworking of our natural bent. We are sinners in act, attitude, spirit and constitution. Forgiveness is necessary. Reformation and right thinking prove to be inadequate and unsatisfactory.

But is forgiveness possible?

Is Forgiveness Possible?

The New Testament teaches that forgiveness is not only necessary, but possible and available to anyone.

What are the requirements of forgiveness? God's part in forgiveness has been completed, for He took the initiative. He was sinned against and realized that man was needy. God, in all of His grace and love, sent His own Son to pay the price for sin. He did for us what we could not do for ourselves.

144

Just because it is possible to be forgiven, we must not think that it is easy for Christ to forgive. It is painful to forgive sins—painful for Christ and painful for us. It was painful for Christ to forgive sin because He took sin seriously. If we condone sin, it is a simple matter to forgive it. But once you take it seriously, it becomes difficult to forgive.

It was painful for Christ to forgive sin because He knew its cost. The cross reminds us that it was not easy even for God to forgive. The nails and spear thrust and the cross represent the ultimate in sacrifice. Jesus went through great turmoil and anguish of soul in the garden before He died. He knew what it meant to forgive sin—it meant His own suffering and death. Forgiveness is offered freely but it is never cheap. Man's part in forgiveness is to admit his sin, to self and to God (see 1 John 1:6,8,10).

For some people to be honest about their need is a big stumbling block. Psychologists tell us that there is little hope for the healing of a patient who doesn't admit that he has a need. It is a well-known fact, for example, that a homosexual cannot be cured of his perversion just because he comes for therapy or counseling. He may simply be going to satisfy his parents, to ease peer pressure or because he is expected to try. Help is still far away. The first step to conquering the problem of the homosexual is for him to admit that he has a need, that he is a sinner. After that he can begin to move in the direction of a new life.

This is true of all sin. If we are to be forgiven, we must admit very candidly to ourselves and to God that we have offended, that we are needy and that we are sinners.

Furthermore, we must confess sin. "If we confess our sins, He is faithful and righteous to forgive us our sins and to cleanse us from all unrighteousness" (1 John 1:9). If we are sincere, He is forgiving and when God forgives He cleanses our life and forgets the sin. God does not keep reminding us of past sin. When He forgives He forgets. The power of Christ to forgive sin is offered to all.

Even Judas, if he had gone to Calvary, if he had waited to see the resurrection and if he had encountered the reason Christ died, could have heard the Saviour say, "Your sins are forgiven!" When God forgives, the burden is lifted, and with it comes great relief!

Bunyan tells the story in his graphic work, *Pilgrim's Progress,* of Christian making his way to the celestial city. He stops when he sees the cross and the burden of his sin falls off his back and rolls down the hill. It gathers speed and rolls into the empty tomb, never to be seen again. When God, through Jesus Christ, forgives our sin, He forgets it.

What are the results of forgiveness? First John 1 tells us that when we are forgiven, we experience:

1. Fellowship—The fellowship of forgiven individuals is with God and with the people of God. There is an intimacy and a oneness that we share when sin, which separates us from God and from each other, is removed. "Indeed our fellowship is with the Father, and with His Son Jesus Christ" (1 John 1:3).

2. Joy—Christians with sin in their lives have a barrier between themselves and the joy that Christ offers. The apostle John wrote about forgiveness and cleansing. "So that our joy may be made complete" (1 John 1:4).

David knew what that was all about. One day he saw the beautiful Bathsheba taking a bath. He paused and lust was born in his heart. It wasn't long before lust was expressed in adultery with Bathsheba. Not only did David lust and commit adultery, but he also saw to it that Bathsheba's husband, Uriah, was put in the front ranks of the army as they went to battle. Uriah's death was indirectly a murder

146

charged to David. Psalm 51 expresses the broken heart of a penitent King David as he poured out his heart to God, "Restore to me the joy of Thy salvation" (Ps. 51:12).

If you are a Christian and there is sin in your life, let me encourage you to confess it and find forgiveness. Our usefulness for Christ is dependent upon a cleansed life. Joy, fellowship and usefulness are available to individuals who have been forgiven. No sin is too great. His grace is greater than all our sin.

Fred Blom was born in Sweden and came to know Christ as his personal Saviour as a lad. He came to America in his teens and fell in with some bad company. His companions led him from one thing to another until one day Fred Blom was behind prison bars for his part in a serious crime. During the lonely weeks in the prison cell, Blom remembered the joy and peace he had earlier experienced when he was serving Christ. He admitted his need, confessed his sin to the Lord and immediately found pardon and new fellowship.

Blom hoped that when his case was reviewed he would be paroled. It did not turn out as he had hoped. His parole was denied because of the seriousness of his crime. He was discouraged but not depressed. He looked at those old iron gates that would never swing open for him and in his mind's eye thought of another set of gates in heaven. From his heart and pen flowed these words, "He the pearly gates will open, so that I might enter in. For He purchased my redemption and forgave me all my sin."[2]

Are you tired of the weight of your sins? Has the guilt become more than you are able to bear? Take Christ at His word, confess your sins and hear His words of assurance, "Your sins are forgiven!"

**Additional Scriptures
to Study About Forgiveness of Sins**
2 Samuel 12:13
Psalms 78:38; 85:2; 103:3; 130:4
Ezekiel 18:21,22
Matthew 6:14,15
Mark 2:5
Acts 13:38,39
Ephesians 1:7
Colossians 2:13
James 5:14-16
1 John 1:9

Footnotes

1. James Stuart Stewart, *A Faith to Proclaim* (New York: Charles Scribner's Sons, 1953), Chapter 2.
2. Story told by Paul Evans in "The Log of the Good Ship Grace," September, 1973.

12. Heaven, Harps and Halos

"I believe in...the life everlasting."

The Apostles' Creed concludes very appropriately. "I believe in the life everlasting." It began, "I believe in God." The two thoughts are related; God made us to live forever.

The Cessation of Physical Life

Physical death is inevitable. Death knocks at the door of every human life. Human history has recorded only two exceptions: Enoch, who "walked with God; and he was not, for God took him" (Gen. 5:24); and Elijah, who "went up by a whirlwind to heaven" (2 Kings 2:11). We may prolong the visit of death, but we cannot elude that inevitable appointment.

Recently a man died at the age of 117 in the southwestern

149

part of the United States. It was a newsworthy event. Rather than living the typical "threescore and ten," he had reached almost sixscore. The newspapers noted at the time of his death that he was the second oldest man in the United States. Recently the news media announced that the life expectancy for Americans is 71 years of age. It is 73 for the Japanese and only 43 years of age for parts of Africa.

But for all people death ultimately comes. There is no way that we can postpone death indefinitely. It is exciting to see life prolonged through organ transplants, proper exercise, adequate rest and proper foods. My dad, who is now 74, had open heart surgery two years ago and had three artery bypasses. Through the years he had watched his weight, he ate the right foods, had taken vitamin supplements, roller skated and ice skated. (His heart malfunction was caused by pressure.) Dad was wise to give attention to his health and prolong his usefulness as a healthy Christian.

All of us who recognize that our body is the temple of the Holy Spirit should be concerned about prolonging our usefulness and our life but there is no guarantee of a long life for anyone. There *is* a guarantee that each one of us will someday face death. The only possible exception in the future is that the Lord's return would precede our death.

The soul is eternal. Job asked the question, "If a man dies, will he live again?" (Job 14:14). A "heavy" question, one that deserves our attention.

Certain tribes of Indians made a practice of burying their dead on hillsides facing the sunrise. Although unacquainted with Christian thought, they had an instinctive belief in a dawn of a better day for the soul.

In the last great act of Shakespeare's *Anthony and Cleopatra,* the queen prepares for the end. Decked in the symbols of her final glory, she awaits a world where they have little

150

worth: "Give me my robe, put on my crown. I have immortal longings in me." Deep within each of us there are these "immortal longings," the knowledge that we were not born for death.

C.S. Lewis brings the subject into focus when he adds, "The Christian says, 'Creatures are not born with desires unless satisfaction for those desires exists.' A baby feels hunger: well, there is such a thing as food. A duckling wants to swim: well, there is such a thing as water . . . If I find in myself a desire which no experience in this world can satisfy, the most probable explanation is that I was made for another world."[1]

The cry of man is that "God has set eternity in our hearts." The Old Testament hints at the fact that man lives forever (see Ps. 16), but the New Testament is explicit: "For what does it profit a man to gain the whole world, and forfeit his soul?" (Mark 8:36). In 1 Corinthians 15 Paul discusses resurrection and eternal life. The soul shall exist eternally with God or in separation from God.

Four False Notions About Eternity

Many false notions keep people from understanding the truth regarding eternity and what God has planned for His people. I would like for you to briefly consider four false notions.

One false notion is that the soul goes first to purgatory. The teaching regarding purgatory is really quite logical. It assumes that a man at death is not prepared to go immediately into heaven. There must be some place of preparation, a place for further cleansing of the life, making it fit for heaven. Although there is some traditional support for the teaching of purgatory, there is no solid *biblical* support for this doctrine.

Not only does the concept of purgatory lack a substantial scriptural foundation, but it fails to reckon with the doctrine of grace. No one in himself is prepared for heaven at the time of death. We are acceptable in the presence of God only through Christ. We are righteous, completely righteous, because He has made us holy.

Just this week a young lady came into my office and wanted to discuss the Christian message. Some of her friends and relatives had recently become Christians and had been sharing their testimony with her. They took a trip together. During the five hours that they were in the car, all they did was talk about the Lord. She was fascinated by what they had to say and was intrigued by the answers they gave to her questions. She hesitated to give her life to Christ because, as she said, "I am not completely ready. I still have to make further preparation." I reminded her that Christ calls us to Himself just as we are. We do not need to be completely ready to be accepted. We must accept the One who is complete.

We discussed the Scriptures, talked further and finally she prayed to receive Christ into her life. At that moment she was ready for heaven. There is no necessity for anyone to go through a period of purging after death so as to be prepared more adequately to be a citizen of God's heaven. We will never be more complete and perfect than we are now. Every Christian is "complete in Him."

Another false notion is that when a Christian dies his soul enters into a period of sleep. Then at the final resurrection day the soul will be revived. There is scriptural support, however, that at the moment of death the believer is ushered immediately and consciously into the presence of his Lord.

One scriptural basis for this assurance is Luke 23:39-43. When Jesus died on the cross He was flanked on either side by thieves. One mocked Him. The other placed his faith in Jesus, and the Master gave him the promise, "Truly I say to you, today you shall be with Me in Paradise" (Luke 23:43). Paul testified, "For to me to live is Christ, and to die is gain" (Phil. 1:21). He then added that he had "the desire to depart and be with Christ" (Phil 1:23). There is no indication in Paul's writings that there is anything but immediate entrance into the presence of Christ when a person departs this life.

A third false notion is that there will be a second chance. Some have taught that because God is love there must be an opportunity for people to re-evaluate their situation and to choose God sometime after death. This theory has a great deal of appeal for those of us who have seen loved ones die in unbelief. The biblical evidence for this position is lacking. According to the Scriptures the state of a believer is settled at the time of death. There is no second chance.

The parable of the rich man and the poor man, Lazarus (Luke 16:19-31), implies that the destiny of a man is determined in this life and there is no opportunity to alter that destiny at some future date. The rich man died in unbelief and went to a place of "torment" (v. 23) and Lazarus, the poor man, went to "Abraham's bosom" (v. 22). The patriarch, Abraham, told the unbelieving rich man, "Between us and you there is a great chasm fixed, in order that those who wish to come over from here to you may not be able, and that none may cross over from there to us" (v. 26). Second Corinthians 5:8 says that when we are "absent from the body" we are "at home with the Lord."

A fourth false notion is that there is no hell. Many, many people cannot believe that God would condemn anyone to a place called hell. In a sense they are right. God condemns no one to hell—they condemn themselves. Individuals choose

153

not to accept Christ's offer of eternal life and God simply confirms their choice!

The teaching of Scripture seems clear. Some are going to heaven, others are going to hell (see Matt. 10:28; Mark 10:21; Luke 12:5). If God is just and the universe is moral, truth and righteousness must reign and the holiness of God must be vindicated. It is not a pleasant prospect, but it is a plain teaching of God's Word. Man's decision will determine his ultimate destiny. He who has trusted in Jesus Christ for salvation, experiences eternal life. This life is here-and-now as well as future.

Eternal Life—Here-and-Now

Jesus said, "I came that they might have life, and might have it abundantly" (John 10:10). John wrote "God has given us eternal life, and this life is in His Son" (1 John 5:11). The apostle was writing to Christians telling them that God had "life-plus," and is a present possession.

Many Christians are confused at this point. They feel that salvation's blessings are restricted to the world to come. But the Bible teaches that eternal life has come in the midst of our every-day life, yes, even the twentieth century world of freeways, astronauts and tranquilizers, "God *has given* us eternal life."

One theologian has spoken of the overlap of the ages, that the age to come has filtered through the age that is now. To put it another way, it might be said that we shall be glorified, but we are beginning to taste glorification now . . . we shall be sanctified, but we are experiencing the beginnings of sanctification now. We shall be redeemed totally, but we are experiencing some of redemption right now.

The blessings of heaven are being tasted on earth. This quality of life begins the moment an individual places faith in Christ and thereby shares His life. We have eternal life—here and now—but it is only a foretaste of its fullness.

God has whetted our appetites for the main course, which has to come later!

When I was a boy, Christmas was an especially exciting time. It was a time of waiting and hoping for certain gifts. Consequently, I did more than my share of snooping at that time of the year!

One year mom had carefully hidden my gifts. One day when she wasn't home, I went through her favorite hiding places and located a gift with my name on it. The minute I saw it I knew what it was: golf clubs. The shape of the package gave it away. When mom wasn't around, I would go and feel the package, shake it and pretend that I was on the golf course. The point is, I was already enjoying the pleasures of a future event, namely the unveiling. It had my name on it. I knew what it was. But only Christmas would reveal it in its fullness.

Have you noticed how often local grocery stores will set up a table hosted by one of their employees or a food company representative. They will offer samples of crackers, eggnog, cheese, sausage or some other tasty morsel and hope that our appetites will be whetted enough to purchase a box or a package of that item.

In a similar way, God gives to the believer a foretaste of what someday will be experienced in its fullness. God's life within us is rooted in the world to come. Not only are we going to live there someday but, through Him and in Him, we have an existence there already.

The Word of God cannot be accused of teaching a "pie in the sky by and by" theology. Rather, it teaches life everlasting which is for now and which is for eternity. Life eternal is far better than a fur coat which can become threadbare, a

Cadillac which can rust out or a Paris trip which is soon over, because what Christ offers is fellowship with God, forgiveness of sins, deep internal peace and the assurance of life everlasting both here and throughout eternity.

Eternal Life—in Heaven

The biblical teaching on life everlasting, the hope of the Christian, revolves around the concept of heaven. In an article, "What's So Great About Heaven?," Calvin Linton pictures a "harp-strumming, bald-headed, ex-businessman with wings, sitting on clouds."[2] This is the concept many have of a person in heaven. What really does the Bible teach about heaven?

Heaven is a place for believers. As Jesus' death became more imminent, the apostles became increasingly depressed. They sensed that they were about to lose a friend. They had spent three years following the miracle-worker and now it was just about over.

Jesus sat these dear men down and told them, "Let not your heart be troubled; believe in God, believe also in Me. In My Father's house are many dwelling places; if it were not so, I would have told you; for I go to prepare a place for you. And if I go and prepare a place for you, I will come again, and receive you to Myself; that where I am, there you may be also" (John 14:1-3). After telling them about the place He was preparing in heaven, He showed them the way, when He shared these beautiful words. "I am the way, and the truth, and the life; no one comes to the Father, but through Me" (John 14:6).

Heaven is a place reserved for Christians.

In an earlier chapter I mentioned that Lindon Karo, a young pastor and a former student, died at the age of 32 from a rare blood cancer. He died in the midst of a series he

156

was preaching on the Apostles' Creed. His wife tells the story of the last few moments of his life.

> We all knew that we were facing the end, and so did Lin. He chided us for our apparent sadness. When Gordy Lindquist came in the room in the early evening, knowing that Lin was dying, Lin said to him, "Why are you guys so gloomy?"
>
> Our grief was shared by the hospital staff. Dr. Tim Gess, Lin's Christian intern, sat at the nursing station most of the afternoon, tears streaming down his face.
>
> About 9:45 that evening, Lin leaned over to me and said, "Good-bye, honey." Then he grabbed Dad's hand and said, "Thanks for coming, Lloyd." And to Emmett, "It's been great, Emmett." A few minutes later he said, "I wanted to go in a blaze of glory, but this is the best I can do." He lapsed into a coma.
>
> Lindon Peder Karo died at 10:40 P.M., March 21, at the age of thirty-two. He did not live to preach the last two sermons, "I Believe in the Resurrection of the Body," and "I Believe in the Life Everlasting." But he is experiencing both.[3]

Heaven has a perfect environment. Most important of all, we shall be with our Lord. The new heaven is described as "the tabernacle of God" that shall be "among men," a place where "God Himself shall be" (Rev. 21:3). All believers shall share in that relationship with our Lord. It is a place without tears, suffering, and sin (Rev. 21:4).

The older I get the better heaven looks. I thought very little about heaven when a boy. I started to think about it somewhat seriously as a teen. But with the passing of adult years I take it more seriously all the time. Many dear friends are now enjoying that place of God's perfect environment. My favorite seminary professor, Edward John Carnell, died

157

prematurely (to my mind!) at the age of 47. He left an indelible mark upon my life. I will never forget his commitment to the Scriptures and his profound method of sharing the truths of theology. I look forward to seeing Dr. Carnell once again.

My Uncle Gust was in his seventies when he died. I assume that he has lost his thick Swedish accent, but I doubt that he has forgotten all those great stories that he could tell by the hour. I like to think that the apostle Peter has slapped his sides more than once listening to Gust tell stories about the old Swedish roofer who was working when the fog set in. When the fog cleared, he had roofed seven feet beyond the peak.

Jana Hammond had just graduated from high school when God called her home. It all seemed so premature to me. Jana had so much to offer to everyone—a kind word, a sweet smile, a thoughtful piece of spiritual advice. God knew best. Jana is with her Lord and someday all her believing friends will be reunited with her. Heaven looks better all the time!

Heaven is beyond our comprehension. Our langauge simply strains to express what that place is going to be like. We can only get a glimpse at best. When John describes it he speaks of its brilliance "like a very costly stone, as a stone of crystal-clear jasper" (Rev. 21:11). The city is made of pure gold (Rev. 21:18). The foundation stones of the city wall are adorned with every imaginable type of precious stone (Rev. 21:19-21). All this talk of gold, precious stones and unimaginable beauty is at best an imperfect conveyer of a perfect state. God can be trusted to provide for His own. Heaven will be better than you and I could ever imagine.

The Chicago Daily News carried the cartoons of Nobel Prize winner, Vaughan Shoemaker, for many years. Each year on the front page of the Christmas Eve edition they carried the same cartoon of a beautifully decorated Christmas tree. Beneath it was an unopened package which was labeled, "Eternal Life." John 3:16 was quoted and the cartoon was entitled, "The Untaken Gift."

We believe in the life everlasting—abundant life, here and now—and life with God eternally. This is no idle whim of pietistic minds. This is no "pie in the sky by and by." This is the confidence of believers. First John 5:12,13 says, "He who has the Son has the life; he who does not have the Son of God does not have the life. These things I have written to you who believe in the name of the Son of God, in order that you may *know* (not think, not hope, not dream but know) that you have eternal life."

Additional Scriptures
to Study About Life Everlasting
Daniel 12:2
Matthew 25:46
Luke 18:28-30
John 3:14-16,36; 4:35,36; 5:24; 6:27,40; 10:27-30; 12:25; 17:1-3
Romans 2:5-7; 6:22,23
Galatians 6:8
Titus 1:1,2
1 John 2:25
Jude 20,21

Footnotes

1. C.S. Lewis, *Mere Christianity* (New York, Macmillan Publishing Company, 1943, 1945, 1956), p. 118.
2. Calvin Linton, "What's So Great About Heaven?" *Christianity Today*, November 20, 1970, p. 160.
3. Karo, *Adventure in Dying*, pp. 210,211.